NO-FAT LOW-FAT
PUDDINGS

NO-FAT LOW-FAT
PUDDINGS

85 INDULGENT COMFORT RECIPES

Divine desserts for everyday eating, including poached fruit, steamed puddings, crumbles, pastries, pancakes and meringues, jellies and soufflés, shown in 425 step-by-step photographs

Edited by Simona Hill

southwater

This edition is published by Southwater,
an imprint of Anness Publishing Ltd, Blaby Road,
Wigston, Leicestershire LE18 4SE

Email: info@anness.com

Web: www.southwaterbooks.com; www.annesspublishing.com

If you like the images in this book and would like to investigate
using them for publishing, promotions or advertising, please visit
our website www.practicalpictures.com for more information.

Publisher: Joanna Lorenz
Editorial Director: Helen Sudell
Editor: Simona Hill
Editorial Reader: Barbara Toft
Production Controller: Christine Ni
Recipes: Catherine Atkinson, Alex Barker, Michelle Berriedale-
Johnson, Angela Boggiano, Janet Brinkworth, Carla Capalbo,
Jacqueline Clark, Frances Cleary, Carol Clements, Roz Denny,
Patrizia Diemling, Nicola Diggins, Joanna Farrow, Christine France,
Sarah Gates, Shirley Gill, Rosamund Grant, Carole Handslip,
Deh-Ta Hsiung, Shehzad Husain, Soheila Kimberley, Gilly Love,
Sue Maggs, Maggie Mayhew, Maggie Parnell, Anne Sheasby,
Liz Trigg, Laura Washburn, Steven Wheeler, Kate Whiteman,
Elizabeth Wolf-Cohen, Jeni Wright
Photographers: William Lingwood, Karl Adamson, Edward Allwright,
David Armstrong, Steve Baxter, James Duncan, Michelle Garrett,
Amanda Heywood, David Jordan, Don Last, Patrick McLeavey,
Michael Michaels, Thomas Odulate

Front cover shows Hot Blackberry and Apple Soufflés – for recipe,
see page 94.

Previously published as part of a larger volume,
Low-fat Guilt-free Desserts

PUBLISHER'S NOTE

Although the advice and information in this book are believed to be
accurate and true at the time of going to press, neither the authors
nor the publisher can accept any legal responsibility or liability
for any errors or omissions that may have been made nor for any
inaccuracies nor for any loss, harm or injury that comes about
from following instructions or advice in this book.

ETHICAL TRADING POLICY

At Anness Publishing we believe that business should be conducted
in an ethical and ecologically sustainable way, with respect for the
environment and a proper regard to the replacement of the natural
resources we employ.

As a publisher, we use a lot of wood pulp in high-quality paper
for printing, and that wood commonly comes from spruce trees.
We are therefore currently growing more than 750,000 trees in three
Scottish forest plantations: Berrymoss (130 hectares/320 acres),
West Touxhill (125 hectares/305 acres) and Deveron Forest
(75 hectares/185 acres). The forests we manage contain more
than 3.5 times the number of trees employed each year in making
paper for the books we manufacture.

Because of this ongoing ecological investment programme, you,
as our customer, can have the pleasure and reassurance of knowing
that a tree is being cultivated on your behalf to naturally replace
the materials used to make the book you are holding.

Our forestry programme is run in accordance with the UK
Woodland Assurance Scheme (UKWAS) and will be certified
by the internationally recognized Forest Stewardship Council (FSC).
The FSC is a non-government organization dedicated to promoting
responsible management of the world's forests. Certification ensures
forests are managed in an environmentally sustainable and socially
responsible way.

For further information, go to www.annesspublishing.com/trees

NOTES

Bracketed terms are intended for American readers.
For all recipes, quantities are given in both metric and imperial
measures and, where appropriate, in standard cups and spoons.
Follow one set of measures, but not a mixture, because they are
not interchangeable.
Standard spoon and cup measures are level.
1 tsp = 5ml, 1 tbsp = 15ml, 1 cup = 250ml/8fl oz.
Australian standard tablespoons are 20ml. Australian readers
should use 3 tsp in place of 1 tbsp for measuring small quantities.
American pints are 16fl oz/2 cups. American readers should use
20fl oz/2.5 cups in place of 1 pint when measuring liquids.
Electric oven temperatures in this book are for conventional ovens.
When using a fan oven, the temperature will probably need to be
reduced by about 10–20°C/20–40°F. Since ovens vary, you should
check with your manufacturer's instruction book for guidance.
The nutritional analysis given for each recipe is calculated per
portion (i.e. serving or item), unless otherwise stated. If the recipe
gives a range, such as Serves 4–6, then the nutritional analysis will
be for the smaller portion size, i.e. 6 servings. The analysis does not
include optional ingredients, such as salt added to taste.
Medium (US large) eggs are used unless otherwise stated.

CONTENTS

INTRODUCTION

A healthy diet that is nutritionally balanced and low in fat and sugar is one that many people aspire to. If you are following a low-fat diet in order to improve your health, or because you want to lose weight, then going without dessert may seem like the sensible option. For those with a sweet tooth, tempting desserts laden with glorious ingredients are often the undoing of good intentions, so if a sweet treat is the highlight of the day and an essential part of mealtimes, then planning ahead and building up a repertoire of low-fat treats that can be made quickly and easily is the answer. Incorporating a little of all the foods that you like into your diet, albeit in small portions, will stop you from feeling deprived and help you to adhere to your plans to change your eating habits for good. If you have a sweet tooth, removing desserts from your diet will result in cravings for the foods that have been denied.

This appealing volume contains 85 delicious low-fat dessert recipes to make that are guaranteed to satisfy any sweet cravings. So, if generous puddings, crumbles, pancakes, cakes, and soufflés are the dishes you desire, then this book contains all that you need. There are desserts for all tastes and occasions, from everyday fruit salads and baked goods, to seasonal and special occasion dishes, such as cinnamon apple gateau and griddle cakes with mulled plums, that look and taste sensational. The recipes are divided according to type, and there are chapters on hot fruit puddings and desserts; cold fruit puddings

and desserts; pastries, pancakes, meringues and cakes; custards, soufflés and whips; and fruit salads, ices and sorbets. Each recipe has been adapted to contain 5g of fat or fewer per portion, making a sweet treat a realistic option every day. All are shown with step-by-step instructions and photographs, and many use standard store-cupboard ingredients that can be rustled up in minutes.

The secret of eating for good health is making sure that your diet has a sound nutritional balance. Cutting down on fat but increasing sugar is not the solution, so while these puddings bring a little sweetness into our lives, many of them do so by using small amounts of honey or the natural sugars present in fresh fruits.

We all know we should be eating more fruit – it is recommended that we eat five portions of fresh fruit or vegetables each day – so fresh fruit desserts score on a variety of levels, not only supplying sweetness, but also contributing fibre, essential vitamins and minerals. Fruit offers a perfect nutrition food package, and they are essential to a well-balanced diet. The addition of different colours of food to the dessert plate adds to its appeal. The recipes in this book make full use of the wonderfully abundant choice of fruits that are available throughout the year, such as apples, bananas and oranges, as well as seasonal plums, apricots and pears which are at their most economical and flavourful in the late summer. When

BELOW: Rice pudding is a traditional favourite brought up to date with a sweet red berry compote.

BELOW: Pancakes are perfect for any time of year. Ring the changes with healthy fruit fillings.

ABOVE: Fruit salads are refreshing and appealing. The natural sugars they contain will satisfy sweet cravings.

ABOVE: Grain-based desserts are always filling and taste delicious served with sweetened fruits.

choices are fewer in the winter, there are plenty of ideas to incorporate dried fruits into recipes to help ring the changes and provide further alternatives.

BEFORE YOU BEGIN

Read through the recipe you have chosen and make sure that you understand the techniques described before beginning, and that you have sufficient time to make the dish. Assemble all the ingredients just to double-check that you have them all. If a dish needs baking, check that you have the correct bakeware – non-stick varieties are ideal and mean that less fat can be used in the preparation of the tin (pan). If a dish needs to be chilled, ensure that you allow enough time for that part of the recipe.

GOOD HABITS TO PRACTISE

• Eating large quantities of a dessert, even if it is low in fat, will not help any weight-loss plan. Watching your portion size and being strict with yourself is the pay-off for being able to eat dessert, so savour a small treat instead.

• When choosing an accompaniment to a dessert, replace high-fat ingredients with healthy lower fat varieties. For example, choose low-fat ice cream, yogurt or cream rather than full-fat versions, and make custard with skimmed milk rather than whole (full-fat) milk. Such additions to a low-fat recipe do make the food more appealing, tasty and satisfying, and when added in small quantities, will ultimately help you stick to your low-fat plan. However, go easy on the quantity, and remember to count the extra calories.

• Choose desserts that have maximum flavour, for example, with a recipe that calls for fruit as the main ingredient, save the recipe until the fruit is at the height of its season to gain added sweetness and the fullest flavour. You'll appreciate the taste much more too. Choosing a fruit recipe helps you to incorporate one of your five-a-day fruit and vegetables into your diet.

• Stewing or poaching fruit in highly flavoured or concentrated ingredients such as citrus juice, vanilla extract, liqueurs or other alcohol adds desirable depth to the flavour of the dessert. Spices also pep up many dishes and provide complementary flavours for other ingredients, such as apples with cinnamon, or rice pudding with nutmeg. Add sugar to poached fruit in moderation, allowing it to be fully incorporated before tasting. Serve them with low-fat yogurt or ice cream.

• Choose desserts that incorporate grains such as rice, semolina or oats because these foods will help you to feel full and satisfied for longer.

• Fruit offers the perfect nutrition option, so eat whole fruit for dessert if you can on some days. It is healthy and sustaining as well as being the ultimate convenience food.

• Presentation is key: a dessert that looks appealing enhances our enjoyment of it. A dusting of icing (confectioners') sugar, or unsweetened cocoa powder, looks attractive – use a tea strainer and keep your hand movements light – or you could use a few berries as plate decorations.

• Light desserts such as mousses, compotes, brûlées and whips are perfect for serving after hearty meals, adding a hint of sweetness to round off a meal without too many extra calories.

USEFUL TECHNIQUES

The following techniques are all used in the recipes that follow, and are highlighted here to provide further clarification.

REMOVING A STONE FROM A FRUIT

Stones (pits) in fruit are inedible and need to be removed. Use a sharp knife to cut through the flesh to the stone and remove the flesh in segments, or cut right around the fruit and holding one half of the fruit in each hand, gently rotate each hand in opposite directions to ease the fruit apart. Use the tip of the knife to remove the stone and discard it.

REMOVING AN APPLE CORE

An apple corer is the best tool to use to remove the core from an apple. Work on a hard surface and press the corer through the centre of the apple. Remove the corer to leave a perfect cylindrical hole ready for filling. To stop the filling from escaping, leave some of the core in place at the base of the apple. Alternatively, use a sharp knife to cut around the core, then ease the core out in sections.

GRATING ZEST

The zest of citrus fruit adds subtle flavour to many dessert recipes. Thoroughly wash and dry any citrus fruit to be grated, in order to remove any wax coating. Buy unwaxed fruit if you can. Use the finest grater and rub the fruit lightly over the surface, taking only zest and not the bitter white pith.

USING A ZESTER

A zester allows for longer and slightly thicker strips of zest to be removed from a fruit's surface. Wash and dry the fruit to remove the wax, then drag the zester over the surface. Use the shreds for decoration. Alternatively, peel the fruit with your hands, then using a very sharp knife and working on a cutting board, carefully remove and discard as much of the white pith from the peel as possible. Slice the peel into very fine strips and set aside.

SEGMENTING AN ORANGE

Peel the orange and remove as much of the white pith as you can from the surface. Hold the orange over a bowl to collect the juice, and with a very sharp knife, carefully cut down each side of the membrane between each orange segment. The process can be a little fiddly but is worth the extra effort. Remove any seeds from the orange segments with a knife.

STEWING FRUIT

Apples, pears, rhubarb, stone fruits and berries can be stewed. Wash, core or peel each fruit as necessary. Chop any large fruit into small pieces and place in a pan. Cook the fruit over a gentle heat, stirring occasionally. The fruit will start to break down and release liquid. Add a few tablespoons of sugar to taste and cook until it dissolves. Serve with yogurt or low-fat ice cream and meringue.

MAKING A FRUIT COULIS

1 Fresh soft fruit, such as summer berries, is ideal to make sauces, coulis and purées for serving with natural (plain) yogurt, meringue or low-fat ice cream. Press soft fresh fruit through a fine sieve (strainer) into a bowl, and discard the seeds and pulp.

2 Transfer the liquid to a pan and bring to the boil, stirring continuously. Cook for 1–2 minutes until smooth and thick. Leave until cold.

3 Spoon some sauce on each plate. Drip cream from a teaspoon to make small dots evenly around the edge. Draw a cocktail stick through the dots to form heart shapes. Scoop sorbet into the centre.

DISSOLVING GELATINE

1 Powdered gelatine is very easy to use and is readily available in larger supermarkets. For every 15ml/1 tbsp of gelatine in the recipe, place 45ml/3 tbsp of very hot water in a small bowl.

2 Holding the bowl steady, sprinkle the powdered gelatine lightly and evenly over the hot liquid. Always add the gelatine to the liquid, never the other way around.

3 Stir until the gelatine has dissolved completely and the liquid is clear, with no visible crystals. You may need to stand the bowl in a pan of hot water. Dip a fork in the liquid to check if there are any granules left to dissolve. Once dissolved, sieve (strain) the liquid.

UNMOULDING A JELLY

1 Have ready a serving plate that has been rinsed with cold water. Shake it but leave it damp – this will make it easier to centre the jelly. Run the tip of a knife around the moulded mixture, to loosen it.

2 Dip the mould into a bowl of hot water. One or two seconds is usually enough – too long and the mixture will start to melt. If the jelly is stuck, dip again. Several short dips are better than one long one.

3 Quickly invert the plate over the mould. Holding mould and plate together, turn both over. Shake firmly to dislodge the jelly; as soon as you feel it drop, lift off the mould. If it does not lift off, give it another shake.

MAKING A MERINGUE

1 Place the egg whites in a completely clean, grease-free bowl. If even a speck of egg yolk is present, you will not be able to beat the whites successfully.

2 Use a balloon whisk in a wide bowl for the greatest volume (egg whites can increase their volume by about eight times), but an electric hand whisk will also do an efficient job.

3 Whisk the whites until they are firm enough to hold either soft or stiff peaks when you lift the whisk (see individual recipes). For stiffly whisked whites, you should be able to hold the bowl upside down without their sliding out. Use as directed in each recipe.

MAKING PANCAKES

1 Sift the flour between bowls several times to gain maximum aeration. Make a well in the centre of the flour. In a separate bowl, beat the eggs, then pour them into the well. Beat thoroughly with a wooden spoon or an electric whisk to incorporate the flour into the egg.

2 Add milk in small quantities to slacken the paste, and continue to beat until there are no lumps in the batter. Gradually beat in all of the milk. Set aside to rest for 20 minutes, then stir.

3 Preheat a pan over a medium heat. Add a light spray of oil to coat the pan. Add a small ladleful of batter and swirl it quickly around the pan to cover it.

4 Cook the pancake for 30–45 seconds, until it has set. Carefully lift the edge with a palette knife; the base of the pancake should have browned lightly. Shake the pan to loosen the pancake, then turn it over or flip it with a quick twist of your wrist.

5 Cook the other side of the pancake for about 30 seconds, then slide the pancake out on to a plate.

6 Make more pancakes in the same way, then stack them between sheets of kitchen paper until ready to serve. Spread them with your chosen filling before rolling them or folding them neatly into triangles.

USING FILO PASTRY

1 Filo pastry has a paper-thin translucent quality and is made without fat. It is perfect for making low-fat desserts, because the cook can add as much or little fat as is required. Filo pastry is delicate and must be covered with a damp cloth to prevent it from drying out.

2 Cut the sheets of pastry to the required size for the recipe.

3 Sheets of pastry are stacked on top of each other and pasted together with a very thin coat of melted fat such as butter, oil, or low-fat spread. Filo can be scrunched and layered into small tart tins (pans) or can be filled and then gathered at the edges to encase the filling.

MAKING A SORBET

1 Put the sugar and water in a medium pan and heat the mixture, stirring, until the sugar has just dissolved.

2 Add pared citrus zests, herbs or spices, depending on your chosen flavouring. Leave to infuse (steep). Strain and cool, then chill well in the refrigerator. Mix with additional flavourings such as fruit juices, or sieved (strained) puréed fruits.

3 Pour the mixture into a plastic or freezerproof container. It should not be more than 4cm/1½in deep. Cover and freeze in the coldest part of the freezer for 4 hours, or until it has partially frozen and ice crystals have begun to form. Beat with a hand-held electric beater.

4 Lightly beat the egg white and stir it into the sorbet. Freeze the sorbet for another 4 hours or until firm enough to scoop.

MAKING A GRANITA

1 Dissolve 50g/2oz sugar in 10floz/300ml/1¼ cups boiling water. Squeeze the juice from six lemons or oranges, or four ruby grapefruit, and mix together.

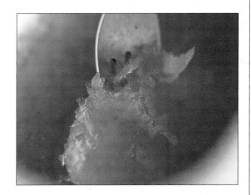

2 Pour the mixture into a freezerproof container. Freeze for 2 hours, until it is mushy around the edges. Beat well with a fork to break up the ice crystals. Return to the freezer and beat it at 30-minute intervals for two hours.

HOT FRUIT PUDDINGS AND DESSERTS

Banish winter chills with warming puddings full of autumn's bountiful harvest of fruits, or add spice

to a late summer evening's alfresco dinner party with a luxurious yet low-fat dessert. Apples, pears,

oranges and peaches have a starring role in many of these puddings. Fat-free and full of flavour,

substantial fruits such as these are filling and nutritious on their own. When topped with crunchy

crumble or sweet batter and flavoured with fragrant nutmeg or cinnamon, for example, they offer a

delightful finale to family dining. From baked apples filled with fruit and spices, to poached pears and

barbecued orange parcels, this chapter contains plenty of recipes that are perfect for those with a sweet tooth.

FRUITY BREAD PUDDING

—

A delicious family favourite from grandmother's kitchen, this filling pud has a lighter, healthier
touch for today. Serve it with natural yogurt.

NUTRITIONAL NOTES

Per portion:

Energy	190Kcals/800kJ
Fat, total	0.89g
Saturated fat	0.21g
Cholesterol	0.75mg
Fibre	1.8g

3 Stir in the bread cubes, mixed spice
and banana slices.

4 Spoon the mixture into a shallow
1.2 litre/2 pint/5 cup ovenproof dish and
pour over the milk.

5 Sprinkle with demerara sugar.

6 Bake for 25–30 minutes, until firm and
golden brown.

7 Serve hot or cold, with natural yogurt
if you like.

INGREDIENTS

75g/3oz/¹/2 cup mixed dried fruit
*150ml/¹/4 pint/²/3 cup unsweetened
apple juice*
*115g/4oz/3–4 slices day-old brown or
white bread, cubed*
5ml/1 tsp mixed (apple pie) spice
1 large banana, sliced
*150ml/¹/4 pint/²/3 cup
skimmed milk*
15ml/1 tbsp demerara (raw) sugar
*low-fat natural (plain) yogurt,
to serve (optional)*

SERVES 4

1 Preheat the oven to 200°C/400°F/
Gas 6.

2 Place the dried fruit in a small pan with
the apple juice, and bring to the boil.
Remove the pan from the heat.

PEACH COBBLER
——

**This delicious cobbler is bursting with late summer flavour. Use ripe peaches for maximum taste
– they are perfectly complemented by the ground almonds in the topping.**

INGREDIENTS
6 large ripe peaches, peeled and sliced
40g/1¹/₂ oz/3 tbsp sugar
30ml/2 tbsp peach brandy
15ml/1 tbsp fresh lemon juice
15ml/1 tbsp cornflour (cornstarch)

FOR THE TOPPING
115g/4oz/1 cup plain (all-purpose) flour
7.5ml/1¹/₂ tsp baking powder
1.5ml/¹/₄ tsp salt
20g/³/₄oz/¹/₄ cup ground almonds
65g/2¹/₂ oz sugar
30ml/2 tbsp low-fat spread
75ml/5 tbsp skimmed milk
1.5ml/¹/₄ tsp almond extract
low-fat custard, to serve (optional)

SERVES 6

1 Preheat the oven to 220°C/425°F/
Gas 7.

2 In a bowl, toss the peaches with the
rest of the main ingredients. Spoon into a
0.5 litre/1 pint baking dish.

3 To make the topping, sift the flour,
baking powder and salt into a bowl. Stir
in the ground almonds and 50g/2oz of the
sugar. With your fingertips or 2 knives
rub or cut in the spread until the mixture
resembles coarse crumbs.

4 Add the milk and almond extract, and
stir until the mixture is just combined.

5 Drop the almond mixture on to the
peaches. Sprinkle with the remaining sugar.

6 Bake for 30–35 minutes in the centre
of the oven, until it is piping hot and the
topping is lightly browned. Serve hot,
with custard, if you like.

NUTRITIONAL NOTES
Per portion:

Energy	393Kcals/1661kJ
Fat, total	4.4g
Saturated fat	0.68g
Cholesterol	0.6mg
Fibre	4g

BAKED APPLES WITH RED WINE

The humble baked apple can be made into a truly special dessert with a delicious filling of
sultanas that have been soaked in spiced red wine.

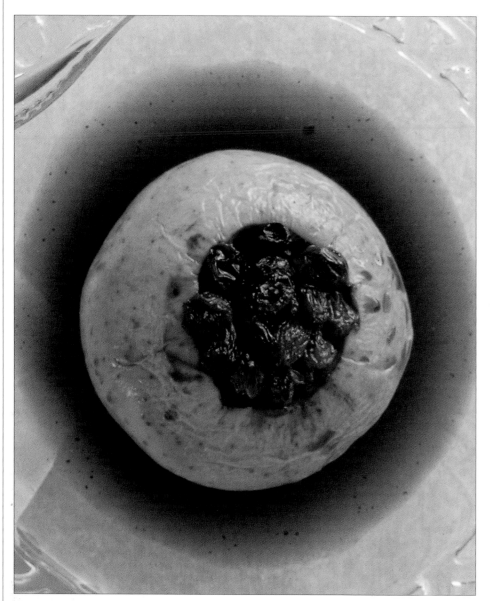

4 Divide the sultana mixture among
the apples. Spoon in a little extra spiced
wine. Arrange the apples in the prepared
baking dish.

5 Pour the rest of the wine around
the apples.

6 Top the filling in each apple with 5ml/
1 tsp of the remaining spread.

7 Bake for 40–50 minutes, or until the
apples are soft but not mushy. Serve hot.

INGREDIENTS
*65g/2¹/2 oz/scant ¹/2 cup sultanas
(golden raisins)
350ml/12fl oz/1¹/2 cups red wine
1.5ml/¹/4 tsp grated nutmeg
1.5ml/¹/4 tsp ground cinnamon
50g/2oz/¹/4 cup sugar
pinch of grated lemon rind
35ml/7 tsp low-fat spread
6 cooking apples*

SERVES 6

1 Put the sultanas in a small bowl and
pour over the wine. Stir in the grated
nutmeg, ground cinnamon, sugar and
lemon rind. Cover and leave to stand for
approximately 1 hour.

2 Preheat the oven to 190°C/375°F/
Gas 5. Use 5ml/1 tsp of the low-fat spread
to grease a baking dish.

3 Remove the core from the apples, but
do not cut right through to the base.

NUTRITIONAL NOTES
Per portion:

Energy	187Kcals/784kJ
Fat, total	2.7g
Saturated fat	0.61g
Cholesterol	0.4mg
Fibre	2.6g

BAKED APPLES WITH APRICOT NUT FILLING

—

A dried fruit and nut filling flavoured with cinnamon makes an interesting combination for an old favourite. Omit the low-fat spread if you want to reduce the fat content further.

INGREDIENTS

75g/3oz/¹/2 cup dried apricots, chopped
20g/³/4 oz/3 tbsp chopped walnuts
5ml/1 tsp grated lemon rind
1.5ml/¹/4 tsp ground cinnamon
115g/4oz/²/3 cup soft light brown sugar
30ml/2 tbsp low-fat spread
6 cooking apples

SERVES 6

1 Preheat the oven to 190°C/375°F/ Gas 5.

2 In a bowl, combine the apricots, walnuts, lemon rind and cinnamon.

3 Add the sugar and rub in two-thirds of the low-fat spread until combined.

4 Remove the core from the apples, but do not cut right through to the base. Peel the top third of each apple.

NUTRITIONAL NOTES
Per portion:

Energy	263Kcals/1095kJ
Fat, total	4.9g
Saturated fat	0.89g
Cholesterol	0.3mg
Fibre	4.3g

5 Widen the top of each apple cavity by about 4cm/1¹/2in to allow for filling. Spoon the filling into the apples.

6 Stand the apples in a baking dish. Trim the base of each if necessary.

7 Melt the remaining low-fat spread and brush it over the apples.

8 Bake for 40–45 minutes or until tender. Serve hot.

DATE, CHOCOLATE AND WALNUT PUDDING

Proper puddings are not totally taboo when you're reducing your fat intake – the trick is to keep the portion sizes small. This one is just within the rules!

3 Place the egg yolk in a heatproof bowl with the vanilla and sugar. Set the bowl over a pan of hot water and whisk until the mixture thickens.

4 Sift the flour and cocoa into the mixture and fold in. Stir in the milk. Whisk the egg whites until thick and fold them in.

5 Spoon the batter into the basin and bake for 40–45 minutes, or until well risen and firm to the touch. Run a knife around the edge then turn it out and serve immediately, with custard if you like.

INGREDIENTS
low-fat spread, for greasing
15g/¹⁄2 oz/1 tbsp chopped walnuts
25g/1oz/2 tbsp chopped dates
1 egg, separated, plus 1 egg white
5ml/1 tsp vanilla extract
30ml/2 tbsp golden caster (superfine) sugar
20g/³⁄4 oz/3 tbsp wholemeal (whole-wheat) flour
15ml/1 tbsp unsweetened cocoa powder
30ml/2 tbsp skimmed milk
low-fat custard, to serve (optional)

SERVES 4

1 Preheat the oven to 180°C/350°F/Gas 4. Grease a 1.2 litre/2 pint/5 cup pudding basin and place a small circle of baking parchment in the base.

2 Put the walnuts and dates in the basin.

NUTRITIONAL NOTES
Per portion:

Energy	126Kcals/530kJ
Fat, total	4.9g
Saturated fat	1.15g
Cholesterol	48.3mg
Fibre	1.3g

SULTANA AND COUSCOUS PUDDINGS

—

Couscous may be better known as a filling savoury side dish, but like other grains, it works perfectly well when combined with sweet ingredients in a dessert.

INGREDIENTS

50g/2oz/1/3 cup sultanas (golden raisins)
475ml/16fl oz/2 cups unsweetened apple juice
90g/31/2 oz/scant 1 cup couscous
2.5ml/1/2 tsp mixed (apple pie) spice
low-fat custard, to serve (optional)

SERVES 4

NUTRITIONAL NOTES

Per portion:

Energy	132Kcals/557kJ
Fat, total	0.4g
Saturated fat	0.09g
Cholesterol	0mg
Fibre	0.3g

1 Lightly grease four 250ml/8fl oz/1 cup pudding basins.

2 Place the sultanas and apple juice in a pan. Bring to the boil, then lower the heat and simmer for 2–3 minutes, to plump up the fruit.

3 Divide half the fruit equally among the four basins and pack it into the bottom of each.

4 Add the couscous and mixed spice to the liquid and fruit in the pan and bring back to the boil, stirring. Cover and leave over a low heat for 8–10 minutes, or until all the liquid has been absorbed.

5 Spoon the couscous into the basins, spread it level, then cover each tightly with foil.

6 Place the basins in a steamer over boiling water, cover and steam for 30 minutes. Run a knife around the edges, Turn the puddings out and serve with custard, if you like.

COOK'S TIP

These puddings can be cooked in the microwave. Use individual microwave-safe basins, cover them and microwave on High for 8–10 minutes.

BLACKBERRY BATTER PUDDING

Light and flavourful fruit compote is topped with a thick pudding that is easy to make and delicious to eat. Nutmeg and lemon adds depth to this dessert.

INGREDIENTS
800g/1¾ lb/7 cups blackberries
45ml/3 tbsp plain (all-purpose) flour
grated rind of 1 lemon
250g/9oz/generous 1 cup sugar
1.5ml/¼ tsp grated nutmeg

FOR THE TOPPING
225g/8oz/2 cups plain (all-purpose) flour
225g/8oz/1 cup sugar
15ml/1 tbsp baking powder
1.5ml/¼ tsp salt
250ml/8fl oz/1 cup
skimmed milk
75g/3oz/6 tbsp low-fat spread, melted

SERVES 8

1 Preheat the oven to 180°C/350°F/ Gas 4.

2 In a large bowl, mix the blackberries with the flour and lemon rind and all but 25g/1oz/2 tbsp of the sugar.

3 Transfer the fruit mixture to a 2 litre/3½ pint/8 cup baking dish.

4 To make the topping, sift the flour, sugar, baking powder and salt into a bowl.

5 In a jug (pitcher), mix the milk and melted low-fat spread.

6 Stir the milk mixture into the dry ingredients and beat until just smooth.

7 Spoon the batter over the berries. Mix the rest of the sugar with the nutmeg, then sprinkle over the pudding.

8 Bake for 50 minutes, until set. Serve hot.

NUTRITIONAL NOTES
Per portion:

Energy	427Kcals/1812kJ
Fat, total	4.5g
Saturated fat	1g
Cholesterol	1.2mg
Fibre	4.1g

FRUIT AND SPICE BREAD PUDDING
—

An easy-to-make fruity dessert with a hint of spice, this is delicious served
either hot or cold. Ring the changes with different fruit throughout the year.

3 Mix together the sultanas, apricots,
sugar and spice and sprinkle half of the
mixture over the bread in the dish.

4 Top with the remaining bread triangles
and then the remaining fruit.

INGREDIENTS
*6 medium slices wholemeal
(whole-wheat) bread*
50g/2oz apricot or strawberry conserve
low-fat spread, for greasing
50g/2oz/¹/3 cup sultanas (golden raisins)
*50g/2oz/¹/4 cup ready-to-eat dried
apricots, chopped*
50g/2oz/¹/3 cup soft light brown sugar
5ml/1 tsp ground mixed (apple pie) spice
2 eggs
*600ml/1 pint/2¹/2 cups
skimmed milk*
finely grated rind of 1 lemon

SERVES 4

1 Preheat the oven to 160°C/325°F/Gas 3.

2 Remove and discard the crusts from the
bread. Spread the slices with jam and cut
into small triangles. Arrange half over the
base of a lightly greased ovenproof dish.

5 Beat the eggs, milk and lemon rind
together. Pour over the bread and leave to
stand for 30 minutes in a cool place.

6 Bake for 45–60 minutes, until lightly
set and golden brown. Serve hot or cold.

NUTRITIONAL NOTES
Per portion:

Energy	305Kcals/1293kJ
Fat, total	4.51g
Saturated fat	1.27g
Cholesterol	99.3mg
Fibre	3.75g

BLACKBERRY AND APPLE CHARLOTTE

A classic pudding that is the perfect reward for an afternoon's blackberry picking.

INGREDIENTS

30ml/2 tbsp low-fat spread
175g/6oz/3 cups fresh white breadcrumbs
50g/2oz/¹/₃ cup soft light brown sugar
60ml/4 tbsp golden (light corn) syrup
finely grated rind and juice of 2 lemons
450g/1lb cooking apples
450g/1lb/4 cups blackberries

SERVES 4

NUTRITIONAL NOTES

Per portion:

Energy	346Kcals/1462kJ
Fat, total	4.2g
Saturated fat	0.74g
Cholesterol	0.5mg
Fibre	6.3g

1 Preheat the oven to 180°C/350°F/Gas 4.

2 Melt the spread in a pan with the breadcrumbs. Sauté for 5–7 minutes, until the crumbs are golden and fairly crisp. Leave to cool slightly.

COOK'S TIP
Pick the ripest berries for best flavour.

3 Heat the sugar, syrup, lemon rind and juice gently in a pan. Add the crumbs and mix well.

4 With a sharp knife, cut the apples in quarters, peel them and remove the cores. Slice the wedges thinly.

5 Arrange a thin layer of blackberries in an ovenproof dish. Top with a thin layer of crumbs, then a thin layer of apple. Add another thin layer of crumbs. Continue until you have used up all the ingredients, finishing with a layer of crumbs.

6 Bake for 30 minutes, until the crumbs are golden and the fruit is soft.

VARIATION
Try other soft berries for this dessert such as raspberries or blackcurrants.

APPLE BROWN BETTY

Cinnamon, cloves and nutmeg, sprinkled over apple, smell delicious while baking in the oven.

INGREDIENTS

50g/2oz/1 cup fresh white breadcrumbs
low-fat spread, for greasing
175g/6oz/1 cup light brown sugar
2.5ml/1/2 tsp ground cinnamon
1.5ml/1/4 tsp ground cloves
1.5ml/1/4 tsp grated nutmeg
900g/2lb eating apples
juice of 1 lemon
30ml/2 tbsp low-fat spread
20g/3/4oz/3 tbsp finely chopped walnuts

SERVES 6

1 Preheat the grill (broiler). Spread the breadcrumbs on a baking sheet and toast until golden. Keep a close watch because they can easily burn. Set aside.

2 Preheat the oven to 190°C/375°F/ Gas 5. Grease a 2 litre/3½ pint/8 cup baking dish.

3 Mix the sugar with the cinnamon, cloves and nutmeg in a bowl.

4 Peel, core and slice the apples. Toss the apple slices with the lemon juice to prevent them from turning brown.

5 Sprinkle about 45ml/3 tbsp of the breadcrumbs over the bottom of the prepared dish. Cover with one-third of the apples and sprinkle one-third of the sugar-spice mixture on top.

6 Add another layer of breadcrumbs and dot with one-quarter of the spread. Repeat the layers twice more, ending with a layer of breadcrumbs. Sprinkle with the nuts, and dot with the remaining spread.

7 Bake for 35–40 minutes, until the apples are tender and the top is golden brown. Serve warm.

NUTRITIONAL NOTES
Per portion:

Energy	257Kcals/1073kJ
Fat, total	4.7g
Saturated fat	0.73g
Cholesterol	0.3mg
Fibre	2.9g

APPLE AND WALNUT CRUMBLE

This is the perfect dessert to make when you have a glut of cooking apples to use up – it will
freeze perfectly too. Serve with plain yogurt or low-fat custard, if you like.

INGREDIENTS

low-fat spread, for greasing
900g/2lb eating apples, peeled, cored
and sliced
grated rind of 1/2 lemon
15ml/1 tbsp fresh lemon juice
115g/4oz/1/2 cup soft light brown sugar
75g/3oz/3/4 cup plain (all-purpose) flour
1.5ml/1/4 tsp salt
1.5ml/1/4 tsp grated nutmeg
2.5ml/1/2 tsp ground cardamom
2.5ml/1/2 tsp ground cinnamon
30ml/2 tbsp low-fat spread
20g/3/4 oz/3 tbsp walnut pieces, chopped

SERVES 6

1 Preheat the oven to 180°C/350°F/
Gas 4. Grease a 23cm/9in oval shallow
baking dish.

2 Toss the apples with the lemon rind
and juice. Arrange them evenly in the
bottom of the prepared dish.

3 In a mixing bowl, combine the sugar,
flour, salt, nutmeg, cardamom and
cinnamon. Rub in the spread until the
mixture resembles coarse crumbs.
Mix in the walnuts.

4 Sprinkle the walnut and spice mixture
evenly over the apples. Cover with foil
and bake for 30 minutes.

5 Remove the foil and continue baking
for about 30 minutes more, until the
apples are tender and the crumble
topping is crisp. Serve warm.

NUTRITIONAL NOTES
Per portion:

Energy	240Kcals/1003kJ
Fat, total	4.7g
Saturated fat	0.76g
Cholesterol	0.3mg
Fibre	3.1g

APPLE COUSCOUS PUDDING

—

This unusual mixture makes a delicious family pudding with a rich fruity flavour, but virtually no fat. You could use pears in place of the apples, or a mixture of the two.

INGREDIENTS
*600ml/1 pint/2¹/₂ cups unsweetened
apple juice
115g/4oz/²/₃ cup couscous
40g/1¹/₂oz/¹/₄ cup sultanas
(golden raisins)
2.5ml/¹/₂ tsp mixed (apple pie) spice
2 large cooking apples
30ml/2 tbsp demerara (raw) sugar
low-fat natural (plain) yogurt, to serve*

SERVES 4

NUTRITIONAL NOTES
Per portion:

Energy	194Kcals/815kJ
Fat, total	0.58g
Saturated fat	0.09g
Cholesterol	0mg
Fibre	0.75g

1 Preheat the oven to 200°C/400°F/Gas 6.

2 Put the apple juice, couscous, sultanas and spice in a pan. Bring to the boil, stirring. Lower the heat, cover and simmer.

COOK'S TIP
Couscous is a pre-cooked wheat that is widely available in supermarkets.

3 Spoon half the couscous mixture into a 1.2 litre/2 pint/5 cup ovenproof dish.

4 Peel, core and slice the apples and arrange half the slices over the couscous. Top with the remaining couscous.

5 Arrange the remaining apple slices on top and sprinkle with the demerara sugar.

6 Bake for 25–30 minutes or until golden brown. Serve hot, with low-fat yogurt.

CHUNKY APPLE BAKE

Unusually, this economical family pudding contains low fat plain cottage cheese, which provides a soft custard-like texture when baked. The muscovado sugar adds depth to the flavour.

INGREDIENTS

450g/1lb cooking apples
75g/3oz wholemeal (whole-wheat) bread,
about 3 slices
115g/4oz/¹/2 cup low-fat cottage
(farmer's) cheese
45ml/3 tbsp light muscovado
(brown) sugar
200ml/7fl oz/scant 1 cup
skimmed milk
5ml/1 tsp demerara (raw) sugar

SERVES 4

NUTRITIONAL NOTES

Per portion:

Energy	158Kcals/669kJ
Fat, total	1g
Saturated fat	0.38g
Cholesterol	2.4mg
Fibre	2.3g

3 Remove the crusts from the bread. Cut the bread into 1cm/½in cubes.

7 Bake for 30–35 minutes, or until the apple bake is golden brown and bubbling. Serve hot.

1 Preheat the oven to 220°C/425°F/Gas 7. Peel the apples, cut them in quarters and remove the cores.

4 Put the apples in a bowl and add the bread cubes, cottage cheese and muscovado sugar. Mix lightly to combine the ingredients, then stir in the skimmed milk.

5 Tip the mixture into a shallow ovenproof dish.

COOK'S TIP

You may need to adjust the amount of milk used, depending on the dryness of the bread; the more stale the bread, the more milk it will absorb. The texture should be very moist but not falling apart.

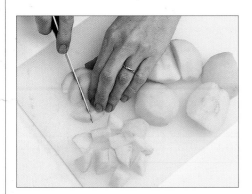

2 Chop the apples into 1cm/½in cubes.

VARIATION

Pears could be used instead of apples.

6 Sprinkle demerara sugar over the top of the mixture.

PLUM, APPLE AND BANANA SCONE PIE

—

**This is one of those simple, satisfying puddings that everyone enjoys. It is delicious hot or cold
and can be served on its own or with low-fat natural yogurt.**

INGREDIENTS
450g/1lb plums
1 cooking apple
1 large banana
150ml/¹/₄ pint/²/₃ cup water
115g/4oz/1 cup wholemeal (whole-wheat)
flour, or half wholemeal and half plain
(all-purpose) flour
10ml/2 tsp baking powder
25g/1oz/3 tbsp raisins
about 60ml/4 tbsp soured milk or low-fat
natural (plain) yogurt
low-fat natural (plain) yogurt,
to serve (optional)

SERVES 4

1 Preheat the oven to 180°C/350°F/Gas 4.

2 Cut the plums in half and ease out the stones (pits) using the tip of a sharp knife. Peel, core and chop the apple, then peel and slice the banana.

NUTRITIONAL NOTES
Per portion:

Energy	195Kcals/831kJ
Fat, total	1g
Saturated fat	0.2g
Cholesterol	0.6mg
Fibre	5.2g

3 Put the fruit in a pan. Pour in the water.

4 Heat the fruit gently and bring to simmering point. Cook slowly for 15 minutes or until the fruit is soft and starting to break down.

5 Spoon the fruit mixture into a pie dish. Level the surface.

6 Mix the flour, baking powder and raisins in a bowl. Add the sour milk or low-fat natural yogurt and mix gently to a very soft dough.

7 Transfer the dough to a lightly floured surface and divide it into 6–8 portions, then pat the portions into flattish scones.

8 Cover the plum and apple mixture with the scones.

9 Bake the pie for 40 minutes until the scone topping is cooked through. Serve the pie hot with natural yogurt, or leave it until cold.

BARBECUED ORANGE PARCELS

This is one of the most delicious ways of rounding off a barbecue party. The oranges taste
wonderful on their own, but can be served with low-fat fromage frais, if you like.

INGREDIENTS
30ml/2 tbsp low-fat spread, plus extra,
melted, for brushing
4 oranges
30ml/2 tbsp maple syrup
30ml/2 tbsp Cointreau or
Grand Marnier liqueur
low-fat fromage frais, to serve (optional)

SERVES 4

1 Cut four double-thickness squares of
foil, large enough to wrap the oranges.

2 Melt about 10ml/2 tsp of low-fat spread
and brush it over the centre of each piece
of foil.

3 Remove some shreds of orange rind, for
the decoration, avoiding the white pith.
Cut them into thin matchsticks using a
very sharp knife. Add to a small pan of
boiling water, for 1 minute, then drain
and dry on kitchen paper.

4 Peel the oranges, removing all the
white pith and the peel. Work over a bowl
so that you can catch the juice.

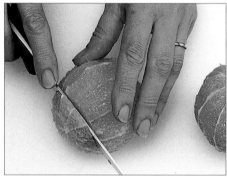

5 With a sharp knife, slice the oranges
crossways into several thick pieces.
Reassemble them and place each orange
on a square of foil.

6 Create a cup shape with the foil by
shaping the foil around the oranges and
leaving the top of the foil standing tall.
This will keep the cups in shape, but
leave the foil open at the top.

7 Mix together the reserved orange juice,
maple syrup and liqueur and spoon the
mixture evenly over the oranges.

8 Add a dab of low-fat spread to each
parcel and fold over the foil, to seal
the cups into packages.

9 Place the parcels on a hot barbecue
for 10–12 minutes, until hot. Handle
them carefully and unwrap using an oven
glove. Serve topped with shreds of orange
rind and fromage frais, if you like.

NUTRITIONAL NOTES
Per portion:

Energy	127Kcals/532kJ
Fat, total	3.2g
Saturated fat	0.74g
Cholesterol	0.5mg
Fibre	2.7g

GRIDDLE CAKES WITH MULLED PLUMS

These wonderfully light little pancakes, with their rich, spicy plum sauce, are intended to be
cooked on the barbecue, but can just as easily be made on the hob.

INGREDIENTS
500g/1¹/₄ lb red plums
90ml/6 tbsp light muscovado
(brown) sugar
1 cinnamon stick
2 whole cloves
1 piece star anise
90ml/6 tbsp unsweetened apple juice
low-fat Greek (US strained plain) yogurt
or fromage frais, to serve (optional)

FOR THE GRIDDLE CAKES
50g/2oz/¹/₂ cup plain (all-purpose) flour
10ml/2 tsp baking powder
pinch of salt
50g/2oz/¹/₂ cup fine cornmeal
30ml/2 tbsp light muscovado
(brown) sugar
1 egg, beaten
300ml/¹/₂ pint/1¹/₄ cups
skimmed milk
15ml/1 tbsp corn oil

SERVES 6

COOK'S TIP
Use spray oil in order to cut the
amount of fat that you use.

1 Halve, carefully stone (pit) and then
quarter the plums.

2 Place the plums in a pan, with the
sugar, spices and apple juice. Bring to
the boil. Lower the heat, cover and
simmer for 8–10 minutes, stirring, until
the plums are soft. Remove the spices.

3 To make the griddle cakes, sift the
flour, baking powder and salt into a bowl
and stir in the cornmeal and sugar.

4 Make a well in the centre of the flour
mixture and add the egg. Beat to form a
smooth batter. Gradually beat in the milk
and 5ml/1 tsp of the oil.

5 Heat a griddle or a heavy frying-pan
over moderate heat. When it is very hot,
brush it with some of the remaining oil
and then drop tablespoons of batter on to
it. Cook the griddle cakes for about a
minute, until bubbles start to appear on
the surface and the underside is golden.

6 Turn the cakes over and cook the other
side for another minute, or until golden.
Bake the other cakes. Serve hot with the
mulled plums. Add a spoonful of low-fat
Greek yogurt or fromage frais, if you like.

NUTRITIONAL NOTES
Per portion:

Energy	159Kcals/669kJ
Fat, total	3.3g
Saturated fat	0.58g
Cholesterol	33.1mg
Fibre	1.7g

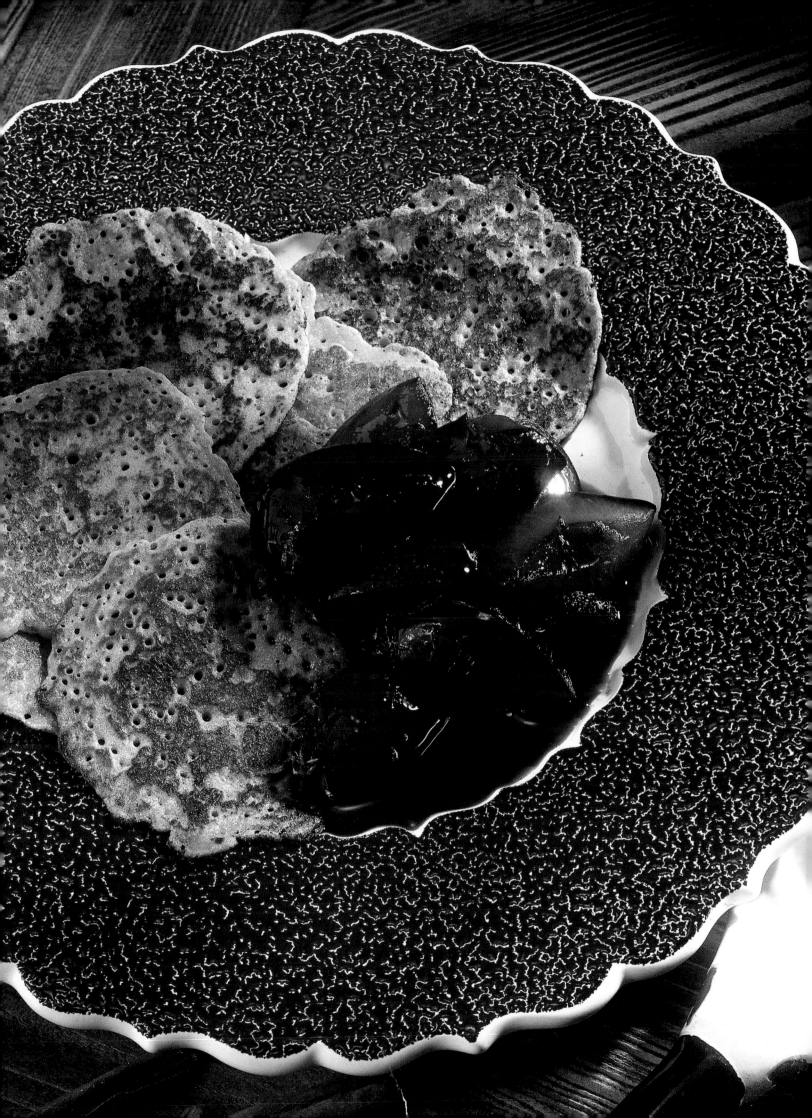

COCONUT DUMPLINGS WITH APRICOT SAUCE

—

These delicate little dumplings are very simple to make and cook in minutes. The sharp flavour
of the sauce offsets the creamy dumplings beautifully.

INGREDIENTS
75g/3oz/6 tbsp low-fat
cottage cheese
1 egg white
15ml/1 tbsp low-fat spread
15ml/1 tbsp light muscovado
(brown) sugar
30ml/2 tbsp self-raising wholemeal
(self-rising whole-wheat) flour
finely grated rind of ¹/2 lemon
15ml/1 tbsp desiccated (dry unsweetened
shredded) coconut, toasted, plus
extra for serving

FOR THE SAUCE
225g/8oz can apricot halves in
natural juice
15ml/1 tbsp lemon juice

SERVES 4

1 Half-fill a steamer with boiling water
and put it on to boil.

NUTRITIONAL NOTES
Per portion:

Energy	112Kcals/470kJ
Fat, total	4.3g
Saturated fat	2.56g
Cholesterol	1.2mg
Fibre	1.7g

2 Meanwhile, in a bowl, beat together the
cottage cheese, egg white and low-fat
spread until they are evenly mixed.

3 Stir in the sugar, flour, lemon rind and
coconut, mixing everything evenly until it
forms a fairly firm dough. The mixture
should be quite stiff but still stirrable; if
it is not stiff enough to hold its shape, stir
in a little more flour.

4 Place 8–12 spoonfuls of the mixture in
the steamer or on the plate, leaving a
space between them.

5 Cover the steamer or pan tightly with
a lid or a plate and steam for about
10 minutes, until the dumplings have
risen and are firm to the touch.

6 To make the sauce, purée the can of
apricots and stir in the lemon juice.

7 Pour into a small pan and heat until
boiling, then serve with the dumplings.
Sprinkle with extra coconut to serve, if
you like.

FANNED POACHED PEARS IN PORT SYRUP

The perfect choice for autumn entertaining, this simple dessert has a beautiful rich colour and
fantastic flavour thanks to the blend of port and lemon.

INGREDIENTS
2 ripe, firm pears
pared rind of 1 lemon
175ml/6fl oz/³/4 cup ruby port
50g/2oz/¹/4 cup caster (superfine) sugar
1 cinnamon stick
60ml/4 tbsp cold water
half-fat crème fraîche, to serve (optional)

TO DECORATE
15ml/1 tbsp sliced hazelnuts, toasted
fresh mint leaves, to decorate

SERVES 4

1 Peel the pears, cut them in half and
remove the cores.

2 Place the lemon rind, port, sugar,
cinnamon stick and water in a pan. Bring
to the boil over a low heat. Add the pears,
lower the heat, cover and poach for 5
minutes. Let the pears cool in the syrup.

3 When the pears are cold, transfer them
to a bowl. Return the syrup to the heat.
Boil rapidly until it has reduced to form a
syrup. Remove the cinnamon stick and
lemon rind and leave the syrup to cool.

4 To serve, place each pear half in turn
cut side down. Keeping it intact at the
stalk end, slice it lengthways, then lift it
off and place on a dessert plate. Press
gently so that the pear fans out.

5 Spoon over the port syrup. Top each
portion with a few hazelnuts and decorate
with mint leaves. Serve with half-fat
crème fraîche, if you like.

NUTRITIONAL NOTES
Per portion:

Energy	173Kcals/725kJ
Fat	2.5g
Saturated fat	0.17g
Cholesterol	0mg
Fibre	1.9g

MULLED PEARS WITH GINGER AND BRANDY

Serve these pears hot or cold, with lightly whipped cream. The flavours improve with keeping,
so you can mull the pears several days before you want to serve them.

INGREDIENTS

600ml/1 pint/2¹/₂ cups red wine
225g/8oz/1 cup caster (superfine) sugar
1 cinnamon stick
6 cloves
finely grated rind of 1 orange
10ml/2 tsp grated fresh root ginger
8 even-sized firm pears, with stalks
15ml/1 tbsp brandy
*25g/1oz/¹/₄ cup flaked (slivered) almonds,
toasted, to decorate*
low-fat whipped cream, to serve (optional)

SERVES 8

1 Put all the ingredients except the
pears, brandy and nuts into a large pan
and heat slowly until the sugar has
dissolved. Simmer for 5 minutes.

2 Peel the pears, leaving the stalks on.
Place upright in the pan. Cover and
simmer until tender, approximately
45–50 minutes, depending on size.

3 Gently remove the pears from the syrup
with a slotted spoon, being very careful
not to dislodge the stalks. Put the cooked
pears in a serving bowl or individual
bowls, if you prefer.

NUTRITIONAL NOTES
Per portion:

Energy	246Kcals/1038kJ
Fat, total	1.9g
Saturated fat	0.13g
Cholesterol	0mg
Fibre	3.5g

4 Boil the syrup until it thickens and
reduces. Cool slightly, add the brandy
and strain over the pears. Decorate with
toasted nuts. Serve with whipped cream,
if you like.

POACHED PEARS IN MAPLE-YOGURT SAUCE

An elegant dessert that is easier to make than it looks – poach the pears in advance, and have the cooled syrup ready to spoon on to the plates just before you serve.

INGREDIENTS
6 firm dessert pears
15ml/1 tbsp lemon juice
250ml/8fl oz/1 cup sweet white wine
or cider
thinly pared rind of 1 lemon
1 cinnamon stick
30ml/2 tbsp maple syrup
2.5ml/1/2 tsp arrowroot
150ml/1/4 pint/2/3 cup low-fat
Greek (US strained plain) yogurt

SERVES 6

1 Peel the pears, leaving them whole and with the stalks. Brush with lemon juice, to prevent them from browning.

2 Use a potato peeler to scoop out the core from the base of each pear.

3 Place the pears in a wide, heavy pan and pour over the wine or cider, with enough cold water to almost cover the pears.

4 Add the lemon rind and cinnamon stick, then bring to the boil. Reduce the heat, cover and simmer gently for 30–40 minutes, or until tender. Turn the pears occasionally so that they cook evenly.

5 Lift out the pears carefully, draining them well. Boil the liquid uncovered to reduce to about 120ml/4fl oz/1/2 cup.

6 Strain into a jug (pitcher) and add the maple syrup. Blend a little of the liquid with the arrowroot in a separate bowl, then return to the jug; mix well.

7 Pour the juice into a pan. Add heat, then stir until thick and clear. Set aside.

COOK'S TIP
The cooking time will vary, depending upon the type of pear and how ripe they are – they should still be firm.

8 Using a sharp knife, evenly slice each pear about three-quarters of the way through from the base, leaving the slices attached at the stem end. Carefully fan each pear out on a serving plate.

9 Once the syrup is cold, stir 30ml/2 tbsp of it into the low-fat Greek yogurt and spoon it around the pears. Drizzle the pears with the remaining syrup and serve immediately.

NUTRITIONAL NOTES
Per portion:

Energy	136Kcals/573kJ
Fat, total	1.4g
Saturated fat	0.79g
Cholesterol	1.8mg
Fibre	3.3g

BLUSHING PEARS

This is a beautiful and impressive dish to serve when entertaining. Pears poached in rosé wine
and sweet spices absorb all the subtle flavours and turn a soft pink colour.

INGREDIENTS

6 firm eating pears
300ml/1/2 pint/11/4 cups rosé wine
150ml/1/4 pint/2/3 cup cranberry juice or
clear apple juice
strip of thinly pared orange rind
1 cinnamon stick
4 whole cloves
1 bay leaf
75ml/5tbsp caster (superfine) sugar
small bay leaves, to decorate

SERVES 6

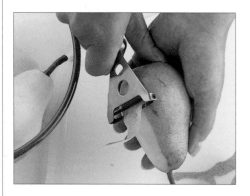

1 Thinly peel the pears with a sharp
knife or vegetable peeler, leaving the
stalks attached.

2 Pour the wine and cranberry or apple
juice into a large heavy pan.

3 Add the orange rind, cinnamon
stick, cloves, bay leaf and sugar. Heat
gently, stirring all the time until the
sugar has dissolved.

4 Add the pears and stand them
upright in the pan. Pour in enough cold
water to barely cover them. Cover and
cook gently over a low heat for 20–30
minutes, or until just tender, turning and
basting occasionally.

5 Using a slotted spoon, gently transfer
the pears to a serving dish.

6 Bring the syrup to the boil and boil
rapidly for 10–15 minutes, or until it has
reduced by half.

7 Strain the syrup and pour over the
pears. Serve hot, decorated with leaves.

COOK'S TIP

Check the pears by piercing with a
skewer or sharp knife towards the end
of the poaching time, because some
may cook more quickly than others.

NUTRITIONAL NOTES
Per portion:

Energy	148Kcals/620kJ
Fat, total	0.16g
Saturated fat	0g
Cholesterol	0mg
Fibre	1.9g

CHAR-GRILLED APPLES ON CINNAMON TOASTS

This yummy treat made with sweet brioches, and fruit coated in cinnamon sugar
makes a fabulous finale to a late summer barbecue.

INGREDIENTS
4 eating apples
juice of 1/2 lemon
4 sweet brioches
15ml/1 tbsp low-fat spread, melted
30ml/2 tbsp golden caster (superfine)
sugar
5ml/1 tsp ground cinnamon
low-fat Greek (US strained plain) yogurt,
to serve (optional)

SERVES 4

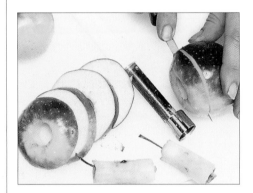

1 Core the apples and cut them
horizontally in three or four thick slices.
Sprinkle with lemon juice.

VARIATION
You could also try pears, peaches or
pineapple for variety. Nutmeg or mixed
spice could also replace the cinnamon.

NUTRITIONAL NOTES
Per portion:

Energy	241Kcals/1016kJ
Fat, total	4.9g
Saturated fat	1.63g
Cholesterol	0.2mg
Fibre	3.0g

2 Cut each brioche into three thick
slices. Brush sparingly with melted low-
fat spread on both sides.

3 Mix together the sugar and ground
cinnamon. Preheat the grill (broiler) if not
using the barbecue.

4 Place the apple and brioche slices in a
single layer on the hot barbecue or under
the grill and cook them for 3–4 minutes,
turning once, until they are beginning to
turn golden brown. Watch them carefully
because they will soon burn.

5 Sprinkle half the cinnamon sugar over
the apple slices and toasts and cook for
1 minute more, until they are a rich
golden brown.

6 To serve, arrange the apple slices over
the toasts and sprinkle them with the
remaining cinnamon sugar. Serve hot,
with low-fat Greek yogurt, if you like.

COOL FRUIT PUDDINGS AND DESSERTS

What could be more refreshing than a luscious fruit dessert that makes the most of fresh

seasonal produce? This chapter of cool dessert and pudding ideas contains a perfect selection for

serving at any time. It includes light recipes filled with stewed and poached fruits that will balance

a hearty main course, or provide a taste of something sweet that is enough to satisfy your cravings.

Choose from light and airy rice pudding served with a thick fruit sauce; a dainty compote, or make an

impressive autumn pudding filled with seasonal fruits. These are just a few of the recipes that will

tempt your palate and help ring the changes. All are extremely low in fat, but taste sensational.

MEXICAN LEMONY RICE PUDDING

Rice pudding is popular the world over and can be made with many flavourings and types of rice. This Mexican version is light and attractive, and is very easy to make.

INGREDIENTS

75g/3oz/¹/2 cup raisins
*90g/3¹/2 oz/¹/2 cup short-grain
(pudding) rice*
2.5cm/1in strip of pared lime rind
250ml/8fl oz/1 cup water
*475ml/16fl oz/2 cups
skimmed milk*
225g/8oz/1 cup sugar
1.5ml/¹/4 tsp salt
2.5cm/1in cinnamon stick
1 egg yolk, well beaten
15ml/1 tbsp low-fat spread
*10ml/2 tsp flaked (slivered) almonds,
toasted, to decorate*
orange segments, to serve

SERVES 4

1 Put the raisins into a small bowl. Cover with warm water and set aside to soak.

2 Put the rice into a pan together with the pared lime or lemon rind and water. Bring slowly to the boil, then lower the heat. Cover the pan and simmer gently for about 20 minutes or until all the water has been absorbed. Remove the rind from the rice and discard it.

3 Add the milk, sugar, salt and cinnamon. Cook, stirring, over a low heat until all the milk has been absorbed. Do not cover.

4 Discard the cinnamon stick. Drain the raisins well.

5 Add the raisins, egg yolk and low-fat spread, stirring constantly until the spread has been absorbed and the pudding is rich and creamy.

6 Pour the rice into a serving dish and allow to cool.

7 Decorate with the toasted flaked almonds and serve with the orange segments.

NUTRITIONAL NOTES

Per portion:

Energy	450Kcals/1903kJ
Fat, total	4.9g
Saturated fat	0.88g
Cholesterol	53mg
Fibre	1.4g

RICE PUDDING WITH MIXED BERRY SAUCE

**A compôte of tart and flavourful red berries contrasts beautifully with traditional
creamy rice pudding for a richly flavoured cool dessert.**

INGREDIENTS
low-fat spread, for greasing
*400g/14oz/2 cups short-grain
(pudding) rice*
*325ml/11fl oz/scant 1¹/2 cups
skimmed milk*
pinch of salt
115g/4oz/²/3 cup soft light brown sugar
5ml/1 tsp vanilla extract
2 eggs, beaten
grated rind of 1 lemon
5ml/1 tsp lemon juice
30ml/2 tbsp low-fat spread
strawberry leaves, to decorate

FOR THE SAUCE
*225g/8oz/2 cups strawberries, hulled
and quartered*
225g/8oz/2 cups raspberries
115g/4oz/¹/2 cup sugar
grated rind of 1 lemon

SERVES 6

1 Preheat the oven to 160°C/325°F/Gas 3.
Grease a deep 2 litre/3¹/2 pint/8 cup
baking dish. Add the rice to boiling water
and boil for 5 minutes. Drain. Transfer
the rice to the prepared baking dish.

2 Combine the milk, salt, brown sugar,
vanilla extract, eggs, and lemon rind and
juice. Pour over the rice and stir.

3 Dot the surface of the rice mixture with
the spread. Bake for about 50 minutes
until the rice is cooked and creamy.

4 Meanwhile, make the sauce. Mix the
berries and sugar in a small pan. Stir over
low heat until the sugar dissolves
completely and the fruit is pulpy.

5 Transfer to a bowl and stir in the lemon
rind. Cool, then chill until required.

6 Remove the rice pudding from the
oven. Leave to cool. Serve with the berry
sauce. Decorate with strawberry leaves,
if you like.

NUTRITIONAL NOTES
Per portion:

Energy	474Kcals/1991kJ
Fat, total	4.9g
Saturated fat	0.95g
Cholesterol	65.5mg
Fibre	1.4g

FRUITED RICE RING

This unusual rice pudding looks beautiful turned out of a ring mould but if you prefer, stir the fruit into the rice and serve in individual dishes.

2 Meanwhile, mix the dried fruit salad and orange juice in a pan and bring to the boil. Cover, then simmer very gently for about 1 hour, until all the liquid is absorbed.

3 Remove the cinnamon stick from the rice and stir in the sugar and orange rind, mixing thoroughly.

4 Arrange the fruit in the base of a lightly oiled 1.5 litre/2½ pint/6¼ cup ring mould. Spoon the rice over, smoothing down firmly. Chill.

5 Run a knife around the edge of the mould and turn out the dessert carefully on to a serving plate.

INGREDIENTS

65g/2½ oz/5 tbsp short-grain (pudding) rice
900ml/1½ pints/3¾ cups semi-skimmed (low-fat) milk
1 cinnamon stick
175g/6oz/1½ cups dried fruit salad
350ml/12fl oz/1½ cups orange juice
45ml/3 tbsp caster (superfine) sugar
finely grated rind of 1 small orange
low-fat oil, for greasing

SERVES 4

1 Mix the rice, milk and cinnamon stick in a large pan and bring to the boil. Lower the heat, cover and simmer, stirring occasionally, for about 1½ hours, until the liquid is absorbed.

VARIATION
Small dried fruits such as currants, sultanas, berries and raisins work well.

NUTRITIONAL NOTES
Per portion:

Energy	343Kcals/1440kJ
Fat, total	4.4g
Saturated fat	2.26g
Cholesterol	15.75mg
Fibre	1.07g

FRESH FRUIT WITH CARAMEL RICE

Creamy rice pudding with a crisp caramel crust sounds wickedly indulgent, but is relatively low
in fat, especially if you serve fairly small portions, with fresh fruit.

INGREDIENTS

*50g/2oz/generous ¼ cup short-grain
(pudding) rice
low-fat spread, for greasing
75ml/5 tbsp demerara (raw) sugar
pinch of salt
400g/14oz can light evaporated milk,
made up to 600ml/1 pint/
2½ cups with water
2 crisp eating apples
1 small fresh pineapple
10ml/2 tsp lemon juice*

SERVES 4

1 Preheat the oven to 150°C/300°F/Gas 2.
Wash the rice under cold water. Drain well
and put into a lightly greased soufflé dish.

2 Add 30ml/2 tbsp of the sugar to the
dish, with the salt. Pour on the diluted
evaporated milk and stir gently. Bake for
2 hours, then leave to cool for 30 minutes.

3 Meanwhile, peel, core and slice the
apples. Peel and slice the pineapple,
then cut it into thin chunks. Toss the fruit
in lemon juice, coating thoroughly, and
set aside.

4 Preheat the grill (broiler). Sprinkle the
remaining sugar over the rice. Grill (broil)
for 5 minutes to caramelize the sugar.
Leave to stand for 5 minutes to harden
the caramel. Serve with the fresh fruit.

NUTRITIONAL NOTES
Per portion:

Energy	309Kcals/1293kJ
Fat, total	4.6g
Saturated fat	2.51g
Cholesterol	34mg
Fibre	2.8g

PEAR AND RASPBERRY COMPOTE

This simple dessert combines seasonal fruit with cinnamon and cloves to make a nutritious dish
that can be eaten on its own or served with low-fat vanilla ice cream.

3 Add the pears to the pan and simmer
gently over a low heat for 15–20 minutes,
or until the pears are tender.

4 Lift out the pears with a slotted spoon
and arrange on a serving dish. Leave
to cool.

5 Meanwhile, remove the cinnamon and
cloves from the syrup in the pan.

6 Blend half the raspberries in a
food processor, then push them through
a sieve (strainer) set over a bowl. Add the
juices to the syrup in the pan. Discard the
pulp in the sieve. Stir in the remaining
raspberries and the raspberry liqueur.

INGREDIENTS

900ml/1½ pint/3¾ cups water
350g/12oz/1¾ cups sugar
1 large cinnamon stick
4–5 whole cloves
900g/2lb pears, peeled, cored and
cut into quarters
275g/10oz/1⅔ cups fresh
raspberries, rinsed
60ml/4 tbsp raspberry liqueur

SERVES 4–6

1 Place the water and sugar in a pan and
heat gently until the sugar dissolves.

2 Add the cinnamon stick and cloves.
Increase the heat and boil for 4 minutes,
stirring, until the mixture is syrupy.

NUTRITIONAL NOTES
Per portion:

Energy	331Kcal/1408kJ
Fat, total	0.3g
Saturated fat	0.1g
Cholesterol	0mg
Fibre	4.8g

7 Pour the sauce over the pears and leave
to cool completely before chilling in the
refrigerator. Alternatively, serve the
compote warm, with low-fat ice cream,
if you like.

AUTUMN PUDDING

—

Summer pudding is far too good to be reserved for the soft fruit season. Here is an autumn version, with apples, plums and blackberries.

INGREDIENTS
450g/1lb eating apples
450g/1lb plums, halved and
stoned (pitted)
225g/8oz/2 cups blackberries
60ml/4 tbsp apple juice
sugar or honey, to sweeten (optional)
8 slices of wholemeal (whole-wheat) bread,
crusts removed
mint sprig and blackberry, to decorate
half-fat crème fraîche, to serve (optional)

SERVES 6

3 Spoon the fruit into the basin. Pour in just enough juice to moisten. Reserve any remaining juice.

4 Cover the fruit completely with the remaining bread. Fit a plate on top, so that it rests on the bread just below the rim. Stand the basin in a larger bowl to catch any juice. Place a weight on the plate and chill overnight.

5 Turn the pudding out on to a plate and pour the reserved juice over any areas that have not absorbed the juice. Decorate with the mint sprig and blackberry. Serve with crème fraîche, if you like.

1 Quarter the apples, remove the cores and peel, then slice them into a pan. Add the plums, blackberries and apple juice. Cover and cook gently for 10–15 minutes until tender.

2 Line the base and sides of a 1.2 litre/ 2 pint/5 cup pudding basin with slices of bread, cut to fit. Press together tightly.

NUTRITIONAL NOTES
Per portion:

Energy	141Kcals/595kJ
Fat, total	1.1g
Saturated fat	0.17g
Cholesterol	0mg
Fibre	5.4g

SEMOLINA FLUMMERY WITH STRAWBERRIES

You can eat this dessert warm or cold, but serve it in small portions because it's filling. This
pudding can be made in advance making it ideal for when you have guests.

2 Mix the semolina with the remaining
milk and stir it into the boiling milk in
the pan. Cook over a medium heat,
stirring constantly, for 3 minutes, until
it thickens.

3 Pour the flummery into four bowls.
If you intend to serve it cold, chill them
for 1–2 hours.

4 Hull the strawberries and cut in half.
Sprinkle the sugar over. Serve the
flummery topped with strawberries.

INGREDIENTS
300ml/¹/2 pint/1¹/4 cups milk
25g/1oz caster (superfine) sugar,
plus extra for sprinkling
pinch of salt
5g/2.5ml vanilla sugar or 2.5ml/
¹/2 tsp vanilla extract
10ml/2 tsp butter
150ml/¹/4 pint/²/3 cup orange juice
40g/1¹/2 oz/¹/4 cup semolina
400g/14oz/3¹/2 cups strawberries

SERVES 4

1 Heat three-quarters of the milk in a
pan, together with the sugar, salt, vanilla
sugar and butter. When the milk comes
to the boil, remove it from the heat and
add the orange juice.

NUTRITIONAL NOTES
Per portion:

Energy	153Kcals/646kJ
Fat, total	3.6g
Saturated fat	2.1g
Cholesterol	10mg
Fibre	1.4g

RASPBERRY MUESLI LAYER

—

As well as being a delicious, low-fat dessert, this can be made in advance
and stored in the refrigerator overnight to be served for a quick, healthy breakfast.

INGREDIENTS

225g/8oz/2 cups fresh or frozen and
thawed raspberries
250ml/8fl oz/1 cup low-fat natural
(plain) yogurt
75g/3oz/¹/2 cup muesli (granola)

SERVES 4

1 Reserve four raspberries for decoration,
then spoon a few raspberries into four
glass dishes.

2 Add a spoonful of yogurt to each glass.

3 Sprinkle a layer of muesli over
the yogurt.

4 Continue the layers until all the
ingredients have been used. Top each
dessert with a whole raspberry.

NUTRITIONAL NOTES
Per portion:

Energy	114Kcals/481kJ
Fat, total	1.7g
Saturated fat	0.48g
Cholesterol	2.3mg
Fibre	2.6g

LINGONBERRY AND SEMOLINA PUDDING

This quick-to-make dessert can be made with different fruits depending upon the season.
It looks pretty served in dainty glass dishes.

2 Put the semolina in the pan and, stirring all the time, return to the boil. Reduce the heat and simmer gently for 5 minutes, until the semolina is cooked. Add the sugar according to taste and the type of fruit used.

3 Turn the mixture into a bowl and, using an electric whisk, whisk for at least 5 minutes until light and frothy. Serve in individual serving dishes and scatter over a few berries to decorate.

INGREDIENTS
1 litre/1³/4 pints/4 cups water
300g/11oz lingonberries, blueberries
or cranberries
150g/5oz/scant 1 cup semolina
about 90g/3¹/2 oz/¹/2 cup caster
(superfine) sugar
fresh berries, to decorate

SERVES 4

1 Wash, dry and pick over the berries, removing stalks and leaves. Put the water and berries in a pan and bring to the boil. Strain the liquid into a clean pan. Discard the berries or push them through a sieve (strainer) into the liquid.

COOK'S TIP
For extra texture and flavour, add extra fresh berries at the end of step 2.

NUTRITIONAL NOTES
Per portion:

Energy	246Kcals/10501kJ
Fat, total	0.8g
Saturated fat	0g
Cholesterol	0mg
Fibre	2g

CLEMENTINES IN CINNAMON CARAMEL
—

**The combination of sweet, yet sharp clementines and caramel sauce with a hint of spice is divine.
Served with low-fat Greek (US strained plain) yogurt, this makes a delicious dessert.**

INGREDIENTS
*8–12 clementines, about 450–500g/
1–1¹/₄ lb
225g/8oz/1 cup sugar
300ml/¹/₂ pint/1¹/₄ cups warm water
2 cinnamon sticks
30ml/2 tbsp orange-flavoured liqueur
25g/1oz/¹/₄ cup shelled, unsalted
pistachio nuts*

SERVES 4

1 Using a vegetable peeler, pare the rind from two clementines and cut it into fine strips. Set aside.

2 Peel the clementines, removing all the pith but keeping each fruit intact. Put the fruits in a heatproof serving bowl.

3 Gently heat the sugar in a pan until it dissolves and turns a rich golden brown. Immediately remove from the heat.

NUTRITIONAL NOTES
Per portion:

Energy	328Kcals/1392kJ
Fat, total	3.5g
Saturated fat	0.42g
Cholesterol	0mg
Fibre	1.4g

4 Pour in the warm water (the mixture will bubble and splutter). Bring slowly to the boil, stirring until all the caramel has dissolved.

5 Add the shredded peel and cinnamon sticks to the pan, then simmer the liquid for 5 minutes. Stir in the orange-flavoured liqueur.

6 Leave the syrup to cool for about 10 minutes, then pour it over the clementines. Cover the bowl, cool, then chill for several hours or overnight.

7 Blanch the pistachio nuts in boiling water. Drain, cool and remove the outer skins. Scatter the nuts over the clementines. Serve immediately.

PASTRIES, PANCAKES MERINGUES AND CAKES

Who would guess that the stunning array of desserts and treats presented in this chapter are low in fat? This collection of irresistible gateaux, light-as-air meringues, fruit-filled pancakes and decadent cheesecakes will impress your guests and provide a wonderful finale to a special occasion or dinner party. Filo pastry is always a treat, with its rich layers and crunchy texture, and here it is perfectly complemented by soft, flavourful, tart fruit and made into individual portions of dessert or a lavish strudel. Filling pancakes and light, airy meringues are flavoured with fruit sauces that make the most of seasonal gluts. Finally, a sumptuous selection of cakes will provide a feast for the eyes as well as the taste buds. Try nectarine Amaretto gateau topped with slices of fruit and syrup, or a baked blackberry cheesecake that is simple to make and tastes divine.

PLUM FILO POCKETS

—

Spiced and sweetened soft cheese-filled plums, baked in filo pastry, provide a wonderful mix of
sweet and savoury tastes for the palate.

INGREDIENTS

115g/4oz/1/2 cup low-fat soft cheese
15ml/1 tbsp light muscovado
(brown) sugar
2.5ml/1/2 tsp ground cloves
8 large, firm plums, halved
and stoned (pitted)
8 sheets filo pastry, thawed, cut in half
sunflower oil, for brushing
icing (confectioners') sugar, for dusting

SERVES 4

1 Preheat the oven to 220°C/425°F/
Gas 7. Mix together the soft cheese, sugar
and ground cloves to make a firm paste.

2 Sandwich the plum halves together with
a spoonful of the cheese mixture.

3 Brush one piece of filo pastry with oil
and place a second diagonally on top.
Repeat with the rest.

4 Place a plum on each filo pastry square,
lift up the sides and pinch the corners
together at the top of the plum. Place the
plums on a baking sheet. Bake for
15–18 minutes, until golden, then dust
with icing sugar.

NUTRITIONAL NOTES
Per portion:

Energy	188Kcals/790kJ
Fat, total	1.87g
Saturated fat	0.27g
Cholesterol	0.29mg
Fibre	2.55g

APRICOT AND PEAR FILO STRUDEL
—

**This is a very quick way of making a strudel – normally, very time-consuming to do –
it tastes delicious all the same! The apricot and pear filling rings the changes.**

INGREDIENTS
*115g/4oz/1/2 cup ready-to-eat dried
apricots, chopped
30ml/2 tbsp apricot conserve
5ml/1 tsp lemon juice
2 pears, peeled, cored and chopped
30ml/2 tbsp flaked (slivered) almonds
50g/2oz/1/3 cup soft light brown sugar
30ml/2 tbsp low-fat spread, melted
8 sheets filo pastry, thawed if frozen
5ml/1 tsp icing (confectioners') sugar,
for dusting*

SERVES 6

1 Put the apricots, apricot conserve,
lemon juice and pears into a pan and heat
for 5–7 minutes. Remove from the heat
and leave to cool.

2 Mix in the flaked almonds and the
sugar until thoroughly combined. Preheat
the oven to 200°C/400°F/Gas 6.

NUTRITIONAL NOTES
Per portion:

Energy	190Kcals/794kJ
Fat, total	4.1g
Saturated fat	0.54g
Cholesterol	0.1mg
Fibre	2.6g

3 Melt the low-fat spread. Lightly grease
a baking sheet. Layer the pastry on the
baking sheet, brushing each layer with
the melted spread.

4 Spoon the filling down the filo, keeping
it to one side of the centre and within
2.5cm/1in of each end.

5 Lift the other side of the pastry up by
sliding a palette knife underneath. Fold
this pastry over the filling. Lift up the
2.5cm/1in end and seal together with
spread. Fold over and seal the ends
neatly. Brush all over with spread again.

6 Bake for 15–20 minutes, until golden.
Dust with icing sugar and serve hot, cut
into diamonds.

APPLE AND BLACKCURRANT PANCAKES

These pancakes are made with a filling but light whole-wheat batter and are topped with a
delicious fruit mixture, a spoonful of crème frâiche and a sprinkling of chopped nuts.

3 Peel and core, then quarter the apples.
Slice them into a pan and add the
blackcurrants and water. Cook over a
gentle heat for 10–15 minutes until the
fruit is soft.

4 Stir in enough demerara sugar
to sweeten.

5 Apply a light, even coat of spray oil to a
pancake pan. Heat the pan, pour in about
30ml/2 tbsp batter, swirl it around and
cook for about 1 minute. Flip the pancake
over with a metal spatula and cook the
other side. Keep the pancake hot while
cooking the remaining pancakes.

6 Fill the pancakes with the apple and
blackcurrant mixture and fold or roll
them up.

7 Serve with a dollop of crème fraîche, if
using, and sprinkle with nuts or sesame
seeds, if you like.

INGREDIENTS
*115g/4oz/1 cup wholemeal
(whole-wheat) flour
300ml/1/2 pint/1 1/4 cups
skimmed milk
1 egg, beaten
15ml/1 tbsp sunflower oil
spray oil, for greasing
half-fat crème fraîche, to serve (optional)
toasted nuts or sesame seeds,
for sprinkling (optional)*

FOR THE FILLING
*450g/1lb cooking apples
225g/8oz/2 cups blackcurrants
30–45ml/2–3 tbsp water
30ml/2 tbsp demerara (raw) sugar*

SERVES 4

1 To make the pancake batter, place the
flour in a mixing bowl and make a well in
the centre.

2 Add a little of the milk with the egg
and the oil. Whisk the flour into the
liquid, then gradually whisk in the rest of
the milk, keeping the batter smooth.
Cover the batter and put it in the
refrigerator while you prepare the filling.

NUTRITIONAL NOTES
Per portion:

Energy	120Kcals/505kJ
Fat, total	3g
Saturated fat	0.5g
Cholesterol	25mg
Fibre	0g

CHERRY PANCAKES

These pancakes are virtually fat-free, lower in calories and higher in fibre than traditional ones.
Serve with a spoonful of natural yogurt or low-fat fromage frais.

INGREDIENTS
50g/2oz/1/2 cup plain (all-purpose) flour
50g/2oz/1/2 cup wholemeal
(whole-wheat) flour
pinch of salt
1 egg white
150ml/1/4 pint/2/3 cup
skimmed milk
150ml/1/4 pint/2/3 cup water
spray oil, for frying

FOR THE FILLING
425g/15oz can black cherries in syrup
7.5ml/1 1/2 tsp arrowroot

SERVES 4

1 Sift the flours and salt into a bowl, adding any bran left in the sieve (strainer). Make a well in the centre of the flour and add the egg white, milk and water. Beat well, then whisk the batter hard until it is smooth and bubbly.

NUTRITIONAL NOTES
Per portion:

Energy	190Kcals/800kJ
Fat, total	1.7g
Saturated fat	0.23g
Cholesterol	0.8mg
Fibre	2.2g

2 Apply a light, even coat of spray oil to a non-stick frying pan. Heat the pan, then pour in a little batter to cover the base, swirling the pan to cover the base evenly.

3 Cook until the pancake is set and golden, then turn to cook the other side. Slide on to kitchen paper and cook the remaining batter, to make eight pancakes.

4 Drain the cherries, reserving the syrup. Mix about 30ml/2 tbsp of the syrup with the arrowroot in a pan. Stir in the rest of the syrup. Heat gently, stirring, until the mixture boils, thickens and clears.

5 Add the cherries and stir until thoroughly heated. Spoon into the pancakes and fold into quarters.

BANANA, MAPLE AND LIME PANCAKES

Pancakes are a treat any day of the week, and they can be made in advance and
stored in the freezer for convenience.

INGREDIENTS
115g/4oz/1 cup plain (all-purpose) flour
1 egg white
250ml/8fl oz/1 cup
skimmed milk
60ml/4 tbsp cold water
spray oil, for frying
shreds of lime rind, to decorate

FOR THE FILLING
4 bananas, sliced
45ml/3 tbsp maple syrup or golden
(light corn) syrup
30ml/2 tbsp fresh lime juice

1 Make the pancake batter by beating
together the flour, egg white, milk and
water in a bowl until smooth and bubbly.
Cover and chill until needed.

2 Apply a light, even coat of spray oil to a
non-stick frying pan. Heat the pan, then
pour in a little batter to coat the base.
Swirl it around the pan to coat evenly.

3 Cook the pancake until golden, then
flip and cook the other side. Slide on to a
plate, cover with foil and keep hot while
making the remaining seven pancakes.

4 To make the filling, mix the bananas,
syrup and lime juice in a pan and simmer
gently for 1 minute. Spoon into the
pancakes and fold into quarters. Sprinkle
with shreds of lime rind to decorate.

NUTRITIONAL NOTES
Per portion:

Energy	282Kcals/1185kJ
Fat, total	2.79g
Saturated fat	0.47g
Cholesterol	1.25mg
Fibre	2.12g

COOK'S TIP
Pancakes freeze well. To store for later
use, interleave them with baking
parchment, wrap and freeze for
up to 3 months.

PANCAKES WITH LEMON AND LIME SAUCE

A tangy, refreshing sauce to end a heavy meal, this goes well with pancakes or fruit tarts
and is the ideal accompaniment for a low-fat orange or mandarin cheesecake.

3 Place all the rind in a pan, cover with water and bring to the boil. Drain the rind through a sieve (strainer) and set it aside.

INGREDIENTS
115g/4oz/1 cup plain (all-purpose) flour
1 egg white
250ml/8fl oz/1 cup skimmed milk
60ml/4 tbsp cold water
spray oil, for frying

FOR THE FILLING
1 lemon
2 limes
50g/2oz/¹/4 cup caster (superfine) sugar
25ml/1¹/2 tbsp arrowroot
300ml/¹/2 pint/1¹/4 cups water
fresh lemon balm or mint leaves, to decorate

SERVES 4

1 To make the pancakes, follow steps 1–3 of the banana, maple and lime pancakes recipe opposite, keeping them warm until the sauce is ready to serve.

2 Using a citrus zester, pare the rind thinly from the lemon and limes. Squeeze the juice from the fruit.

NUTRITIONAL NOTES
Per portion:

Energy	75Kcals/317kJ
Fat, total	0.1g
Saturated fat	0g
Cholesterol	0mg
Fibre	0g

4 In a small bowl, mix a little sugar with the arrowroot. Stir in enough water to give a smooth paste. Heat the remaining water, pour in the arrowroot, and stir constantly until the sauce boils and thickens.

5 Stir in the remaining sugar, the citrus juice and the reserved rind. Serve hot with the pancakes. Decorate with lemon balm or mint.

FLOATING ISLANDS IN HOT PLUM SAUCE

An unusual, low-fat pudding that is simpler to make than it looks. The plum sauce can be made
in advance, and reheated just before you cook the meringues.

INGREDIENTS
450g/1lb red plums
300ml/¹/2 pint/1¹/4 cups unsweetened
apple juice
2 egg whites
30ml/2 tbsp concentrated apple juice
freshly grated nutmeg

SERVES 4

1 Halve the plums and discard the stones
(pits). Place them in a wide pan with the
unsweetened apple juice.

2 Bring to the boil, lower the heat, cover
and simmer gently for 15–20 minutes or
until the plums are tender.

COOK'S TIP
A bottle of concentrated apple juice
is a useful sweetener, but if you don't
have any, use a little honey instead.

3 Meanwhile, place the egg whites in a
grease-free bowl and whisk them until
they hold soft peaks.

4 Gradually whisk in the concentrated
apple juice, whisking until the meringue
holds fairly firm peaks.

VARIATION
Use a fruit liqueur such as Calvados,
apricot brandy or Grand Marnier
instead of the concentrated apple juice.

NUTRITIONAL NOTES
Per portion:

Energy	77Kcals/324kJ
Fat, total	0.3g
Saturated fat	0g
Cholesterol	0mg
Fibre	1.7g

5 Using a tablespoon, scoop the meringue
mixture into the gently simmering plum
sauce. You may need to cook the 'islands'
in two batches.

6 Cover and allow to simmer gently for
2–3 minutes, until the meringues are just
set. Serve immediately, sprinkled with a
little freshly grated nutmeg.

BLACKBERRY BROWN SUGAR MERINGUE

—

**A brown sugar meringue looks very effective, especially when contrasted
with a dark topping. Meringue contains very little fat but is intensely sweet.**

INGREDIENTS
175g/6oz/1 cup soft light brown sugar
3 egg whites
5ml/1 tsp distilled malt vinegar
2.5ml/¹/2 tsp vanilla extract

FOR THE TOPPING
30ml/2 tbsp crème de cassis
350g/12oz/3 cups blackberries
15ml/1 tbsp icing (confectioners')
sugar, sifted
300ml/¹/2 pint/1¹/4 cups low-fat
Greek (US strained plain) yogurt
small blackberry leaves, to decorate
(optional)

SERVES 6

1 Preheat the oven to 160°C/325°F/Gas 3.
Draw a 20cm/8in circle on a sheet of
baking parchment, turn it over and place
on a baking sheet.

2 Spread out the brown sugar on a second
baking sheet and dry in the oven for
8–10 minutes. Sift to remove lumps.

3 Whisk the egg whites in a clean grease-
free bowl until stiff. Add half the dried
brown sugar, 15ml/1 tbsp at a time,
whisking well after each addition. Add
the vinegar and vanilla extract, then fold
in the remaining sugar.

NUTRITIONAL NOTES
Per portion:

Energy	199Kcals/833kJ
Fat, total	2.6g
Saturated fat	1.58g
Cholesterol	3.5mg
Fibre	1.8g

4 Spoon the meringue on to the circle,
leaving a central hollow. Bake for
45 minutes, then turn off the oven, but
leave the meringue in the oven with the
door slightly open, until cold.

5 To make the topping, put the blackberries in a bowl and sprinkle crème de
cassis over them. Leave for 30 minutes.

6 When the meringue is cold, carefully
peel off the baking parchment and
transfer the meringue to a serving plate.
Stir the icing sugar into the low-fat Greek
yogurt and spoon into the centre.

7 Top with the blackberries and decorate
with small blackberry leaves, if you like.
Serve immediately.

APRICOT AND ALMOND CAKE

These moist apricot and almond bars are irresistible low-fat snacks or treats that are perfect for putting in lunchboxes or to share with friends for afternoon tea.

INGREDIENTS

*250g/8oz/2 cups self-raising
(self-rising) flour*
150g/5oz/²⁄3 cup soft light brown sugar
50g/2oz/¹⁄3 cup semolina
175g/6oz/1 cup dried apricots, chopped
2 eggs
30ml/2 tbsp malt extract
30ml/2 tbsp honey
4 fl oz/¹⁄2 pint skimmed milk
2 fl oz/¹⁄4 pint sunflower oil
few drops of almond extract
2 tbsp flaked (slivered) almonds

MAKES 18

1 Preheat the oven to 160°C/325°F/Gas 3. Grease and line a 33 x 18cm/11 x 7in shallow baking tin (pan) and set aside.

2 Sift the flour into a bowl and add the sugar, semolina, dried apricots, eggs, malt extract, honey, milk, oil and almond extract. Mix well until smooth.

NUTRITIONAL NOTES
Per portion:

Energy	153cals
Total fat	4.56g
Saturated fat	0.61mg
Cholesterol	21.5mg
Fibre	1.27g

2 Transfer the mixture to the prepared pan, spread to the edges and sprinkle with the almonds.

COOK'S TIP
Allow the eggs to come to room temperature before using them.

3 Bake for 30–35 minutes or until the centre of the cake springs back when lightly pressed. Turn out on to a wire rack and leave to cool.

4 Remove and discard the lining paper, place the cake on a board and cut it into 18 slices with a sharp knife. Store in an airtight container.

NECTARINE AMARETTO CAKE

Try this delicious Italian-style cake served with a little low-fat sour cream for dessert, or serve it solo for an afternoon treat. The syrup makes it deliciously moist but not soggy.

INGREDIENTS

3 eggs, separated
175g/6oz/³⁄4 cup caster (superfine) sugar
grated rind and juice of 1 lemon
50g/2oz/¹⁄3 cup semolina
40g/1¹⁄2 oz/¹⁄3 cup ground almonds
25g/1oz/¹⁄4 cup plain (all-purpose) flour
2 nectarines or peaches, halved
and stoned (pitted)
60ml/4 tbsp apricot glaze

FOR THE SYRUP

75g/3oz/6 tbsp caster (superfine) sugar
90ml/6 tbsp water
30ml/2 tbsp Amaretto liqueur

1 Preheat the oven to 180°C/350°F/Gas 4. Grease a 20cm/8in round loose-based cake tin (pan). Whisk the egg yolks, caster sugar, lemon rind and juice in a bowl until thick, pale and creamy.

2 Fold in the semolina, almonds and flour until smooth.

3 Whisk the egg whites in a grease-free bowl until fairly stiff.

4 Using a metal spoon, stir a generous spoonful of the whites into the semolina mixture to lighten it, then fold in the remaining egg whites.

5 Spoon the mixture into the prepared cake tin. Bake for 30–35 minutes until the centre of the cake springs back when lightly pressed.

6 Leave to cool slightly then carefully loosen around the cake edge with a metal spatula. Prick the top of the cake with a skewer.

COOK'S TIP

Choose very ripe fruits for this cake because they have more flavour and are sweeter than unripe fruits.

---

7 To make the syrup, heat the sugar and water in a small pan, stirring until dissolved. Boil without stirring for 2 minutes.

8 Add the Amaretto liqueur to the syrup and drizzle slowly over the cake.

9 Remove the cake from the tin and transfer it to a serving plate.

10 Slice the nectarines or peaches, arrange them over the top and brush with the warm apricot glaze.

NUTRITIONAL NOTES
Per portion:

Energy	264Kcals/1108kJ
Fat, total	5.7g
Saturated fat	0.8g
Cholesterol	72.19mg
Fibre	1.1g

CHOCOLATE AND ORANGE ANGEL CAKE

This light-as-air cocoa sponge with its fluffy meringue-like icing is virtually fat free,
yet it tastes heavenly and looks great too.

INGREDIENTS
25g/1oz/¼ cup plain (all-purpose) flour
15g/½ oz reduced-fat cocoa powder
30ml/2 tbsp cornflour (cornstarch)
1.5ml/¼ tsp salt
5 egg whites
2.5ml/½ tsp cream of tartar
115g/4oz/½ cup caster (superfine) sugar
pared rind of 1 orange, blanched,
to decorate

FOR THE ICING
200g/7oz/scant 1 cup caster
(superfine) sugar
1 egg white

SERVES 10

1 Preheat the oven to 180°C/350°F/Gas 4.

2 Beat the egg whites in a clean grease-free bowl until foamy. Add the cream of tartar, then whisk until soft peaks form.

NUTRITIONAL NOTES
Per portion:

Energy	153Kcals/644kJ
Fat, total	0.27g
Saturated fat	0.13g
Cholesterol	0mg
Fibre	0.25g

3 Add the caster sugar to the egg whites a spoonful at a time, whisking for a few minutes after each addition.

4 Into another bowl, sift the flour, cocoa powder, cornflour and salt together three times, to get the maximum amout of air into the flour and cocoa mixture.

5 Sift a third of the flour and cocoa mixture again over the meringue and gently fold in with a metal spatula. Repeat the procedure, sifting and folding in the flour and cocoa mixture twice more.

5 Spoon the mixture into a non-stick 20cm/8in ring mould and level the top.

6 Bake for 35 minutes or until springy when lightly pressed. Leave to set for 10 minutes, then turn upside-down on to a wire rack and leave to cool in the mould. Lift off the mould once cool.

7 To make the icing, put the sugar in a pan with the 75ml/5 tbsp cold water. Stir over a low heat until dissolved. Boil until the syrup reaches 120°C/250°F on a sugar thermometer, or when a drop of the syrup makes a soft ball when dropped into a cup of cold water. Remove from the heat.

8 Whisk the egg white in a grease-free bowl until soft peaks occur. Add the syrup in a thin stream, whisking all the time. Continue to whisk until the mixture is very thick and fluffy.

9 Spread the icing over the top and sides of the cooled cake. Sprinkle the orange rind over the top of the cake and serve.

COOK'S TIP
Do not over-beat the egg whites. They should form soft peaks, so that the air bubbles can expand during cooking.

CINNAMON APPLE GATEAU

Make this lovely cake for an autumn celebration when apples are at their best. It looks stunning and is perfect to serve for a celebration. Serve with low-fat fromage frais or ricotta cheese.

INGREDIENTS
3 eggs
115g/4oz/¹/2 cup caster
(superfine) sugar
75g/3oz/³/4 cup plain
(all-purpose) flour
5ml/1 tsp ground cinnamon

FOR THE FILLING AND TOPPING
4 large eating apples
60ml/4 tbsp clear honey
15ml/1 tbsp water
75g/3oz/¹/2 cup sultanas
(golden raisins)
2.5ml/¹/2 tsp ground cinnamon
350g/12oz/1¹/2 cups low-fat soft cheese
60ml/4 tbsp low-fat fromage frais
10ml/2 tsp lemon juice
45ml/3 tbsp apricot jam, warmed
and strained
fresh mint sprigs, to decorate

SERVES 8

1 Preheat the oven to 190°C/375°F/ Gas 5. Grease and line a 23cm/9in sandwich tin (pan).

2 Place the eggs and caster sugar in a bowl and whisk until thick and mousse-like (when the whisk is lifted, a trail should remain on the surface of the mixture for at least 15 seconds).

3 Sift the flour and cinnamon over the egg mixture. Fold in with a metal spoon.

4 Pour into the prepared tin and bake for 25–30 minutes or until the cake springs back when lightly pressed. Loosen the edge of the cake from the tin, then turn the cake on to a wire rack to cool.

5 To make the filling, peel, core and slice three of the apples and put them in a pan.

6 Add 30ml/2 tbsp of the honey and the water. Cover and cook over a gentle heat for about 10 minutes until the apples have softened. Add the sultanas and cinnamon, stir well, replace the lid and leave to cool.

7 Put the soft cheese in a bowl with the remaining honey, the fromage frais and half the lemon juice. Beat until the mixture is smooth.

8 Halve the cake horizontally; place one half on a board and drizzle over any liquid from the apple mixture. Spread with two-thirds of the cheese mixture, then top with the apple filling. Fit the top of the cake in place.

9 Swirl the remaining cheese mixture over the cake top. Core and slice the remaining apple, sprinkle with the remaining lemon juice and use to decorate the cake edge. Brush the apple with apricot jam and decorate with mint sprigs.

NUTRITIONAL NOTES
Per portion:

Energy	244Kcals/1023kJ
Fat, total	4.05g
Saturated fat	1.71g
Cholesterol	77.95mg
Fibre	1.5g

APRICOT AND ORANGE ROULADE

This elegant dessert is very low in fat and is also perfect for entertaining. It tastes delicious with a spoonful of low-fat Greek yogurt or fromage frais.

INGREDIENTS
low-fat spread, for greasing
4 egg whites
115g/4oz/¹/₂ cup golden caster
(superfine) sugar
50g/2oz/¹/₂ cup plain (all-purpose) flour
finely grated rind of 1 small orange
45ml/3 tbsp orange juice

FOR THE FILLING
115g/4oz/¹/₂ cup ready-to-eat dried
apricots, roughly chopped
150ml/¹/₄ pint/²/₃ cup orange juice

TO DECORATE
10ml/2 tsp icing (confectioners')
sugar, for sprinkling
shreds of pared orange rind, to decorate

SERVES 6

1 Preheat the oven to 200°C/400°F/Gas 6.

2 Grease a 23 × 33cm/9 × 13in Swiss-roll tin (jelly roll) and line it with baking parchment. Grease the paper.

COOK'S TIP
Bake the sponge a day in advance and store it, rolled with the paper, in a cool place.

3 Place the egg whites in a large grease-free bowl and whisk them until they hold soft peaks. Gradually add the sugar, whisking hard after each addition.

4 Fold in the flour, orange rind and juice. Spoon the mixture into the prepared tin and spread it evenly.

5 Bake for 15–18 minutes, or until the sponge is firm and pale gold in colour. Turn out on to a sheet of baking parchment, and roll it up loosely from one short side. Leave to cool.

6 To make the filling, place the apricots in a pan with the orange juice. Cover the pan and leave to simmer until most of the liquid has been absorbed. Purée the apricots in a food processor.

7 Unroll the sponge and spread with the apricot mixture. Roll up the roulade.

8 Arrange strips of paper diagonally across the roll, sprinkle lightly with lines of icing sugar, remove the paper and scatter with shreds of pared orange rind.

NUTRITIONAL NOTES
Per portion:

Energy	154Kcals/652kJ
Fat, total	0.3g
Saturated fat	0.01g
Cholesterol	0mg
Fibre	1.5g

TIA MARIA GATEAU

A feather-light coffee sponge is made extra-special by a creamy liqueur-flavoured filling. A hint
of ginger adds heat and complements the flavour of the coffee.

INGREDIENTS
low-fat spread, for greasing
75g/3oz/³/4 cup plain (all-purpose) flour
30ml/2 tbsp instant coffee powder
3 eggs
115g/4oz/¹/2 cup caster (superfine) sugar
coffee beans, to decorate (optional)

FOR THE FILLING
175g/6oz/³/4 cup low-fat soft cheese
15ml/1 tbsp clear honey
15ml/1 tbsp Tia Maria
50g/2oz/¹/4 cup stem ginger,
roughly chopped

FOR THE ICING
225g/8oz/2 cups icing (confectioners')
sugar, sifted
10ml/2 tsp coffee extract
15ml/1 tbsp water
5ml/1 tsp unsweetened reduced-fat
cocoa powder
coffee beans, to decorate

SERVES 8

1 Preheat the oven to 190°C/375°F/Gas 5.
Grease and line a 20cm/8in deep round
cake tin (pan) with baking parchment.

2 Sift the flour and coffee powder
together on to a sheet of baking
parchment.

3 Whisk the eggs and sugar in a bowl
until thick and mousse-like (when the
whisk is lifted, a trail should remain on
the surface for 10–15 seconds).

4 Gently fold in the flour mixture with a
metal spoon, being careful not to knock
out any air. Turn the mixture into the
prepared tin.

5 Bake the sponge for 30–35 minutes or
until it springs back when lightly pressed.

6 Turn the cake out on to a wire rack and
leave to cool completely. When cold, cut
the cake in half horizontally. Put the
bottom half on a serving plate.

7 To make the filling, mix the soft cheese
with the honey in a bowl. Beat until
smooth, then stir in the Tia Maria and
the chopped stem ginger.

8 Spread the filling over the bottom half
of the cake. Top with the other cake half.

9 To make the icing, mix the icing sugar
and coffee extract with enough of the
water to make an icing that will coat the
back of a wooden spoon. Spread three-
quarters of the icing over the cake.

10 Stir the cocoa into the remaining
icing. Spoon into a piping (pastry) bag.
Cut off the tip and pipe the mocha icing
over the cake. Decorate with coffee beans.

NUTRITIONAL NOTES
Per portion:

Energy	226Kcals/951kJ
Fat, total	3.14g
Saturated fat	1.17g
Cholesterol	75.03mg
Fibre	0.64g

BAKED BLACKBERRY CHEESECAKE

This light, low-fat cheesecake is best made with wild blackberries, but cultivated ones will do; alernatively, substitute other soft fruit, such as loganberries, raspberries or blueberries.

INGREDIENTS
low-fat spread, for greasing
175g/6oz/3/4 cup low-fat
cottage cheese
150ml/1/4 pint/2/3 cup low-fat
natural (plain) yogurt
15ml/1 tbsp wholemeal
(whole-wheat) flour
25g/1oz/2 tbsp golden caster
(superfine) sugar
1 egg and 1 egg white
finely grated rind and juice of 1/2 lemon
200g/7oz/13/4 cups fresh or thawed
frozen blackberries

SERVES 5

1 Preheat the oven to 180°C/350°F/Gas 4. Lightly grease and line the base of an 18cm/7in sandwich cake tin (pan).

2 Place the cottage cheese in a food processor and process until smooth, or push through a sieve (strainer).

3 Stir in the yogurt, flour, sugar, egg and egg white. Add the lemon rind, juice and blackberries, reserving a few for decoration.

4 Pour the mixture into the prepared tin and bake it for 30–35 minutes, or until it is just set. Turn off the oven and leave in the oven for a further 30 minutes.

5 Run a knife around the edge of the cheesecake, and then turn it out. Remove the lining paper.

6 Decorate the cheesecake with the reserved blackberries, and serve warm.

COOK'S TIP
If fresh blackberries are not in season, use canned blackberries in natural juice. Drain the fruit well before adding it to the cheesecake mixture.

NUTRITIONAL NOTES
Per portion:

Energy	95Kcals/402kJ
Fat, total	1.9g
Saturated fat	0.77g
Cholesterol	41.5mg
Fibre	1.4g

JELLIES, CUSTARDS, SOUFFLES AND WHIPS

Creamy and light, yet satisfying and full of flavour, these desserts are ideal to serve

after a rich main course to tantalise the taste buds with their slightly acidic qualities. Grapes,

clementines and oranges add refreshing notes to cold, fragrant jellies. Dried fruit

thickened into a "soup" makes a traditional northern European dessert that is full

of favourite flavours. If your taste is for something creamier and more subtle,

try classic Italian zabaglione with its warm, alcoholic hints. To complete the

chapter an unusual and decadent collection of soufflés and whips are presented. Souffléd rice

pudding is a warming and nostalgic treat that is perfect to serve to the family, while the

apple and blackberry soufflés look sensational enough to serve at a dinner party.

GRAPES IN GRAPE-YOGURT JELLY

This light, refreshing combination makes a great special-occasion dessert. It looks stylish, but takes very little time to make. It is perfect to serve after a substantial meal.

INGREDIENTS

200g/7oz/1¾ cups white seedless grapes
450ml/¾ pint/scant 2 cups unsweetened
white grape juice
15ml/1 tbsp powdered gelatine
120ml/4fl oz/½ cup low-fat
natural (plain) yogurt

SERVES 4

1 Set aside four tiny bunches of grapes for decoration. Pull the rest off their stalks and cut them in half.

2 Divide the grapes among four stemmed glasses and tilt the glasses on one side, propping them firmly in a bowl of ice.

3 Place the grape juice in a pan and heat it until almost boiling. Remove it from the heat and sprinkle the gelatine over the surface, stirring to dissolve the gelatine.

4 Pour half the grape juice over the grapes and leave to set.

5 Cool the remaining grape juice, then stir in the low-fat natural yogurt.

6 Stand the glasses upright and pour in the yogurt mixture. Chill to set, then decorate each glass with grapes.

NUTRITIONAL NOTES
Per portion:

Energy	113Kcals/480kJ
Fat, total	0.4g
Saturated fat	0.16g
Cholesterol	1.3mg
Fibre	0g

CLEMENTINE JELLY

—

Jelly isn't only for children; this adult version has a clear fruity taste and can be made extra special by adding a little white rum or Cointreau.

INGREDIENTS
12 clementines
clear unsweetened white grape juice
(see method for amount)
15ml/1 tbsp powdered gelatine
30ml/2 tbsp caster (superfine) sugar
60ml/4 tbsp half-fat crème fraîche,
for topping

SERVES 4

1 Squeeze the juice from eight of the clementines and pour it into a jug.

2 Make up to 600ml/1 pint/2½ cups with the grape juice, then strain the juice mixture through a fine sieve (strainer).

3 Pour half the juice mixture into a pan. Sprinkle the gelatine on top, leave for 5 minutes, then heat gently until the gelatine has dissolved. Stir in the sugar, then the remaining juice; set aside.

NUTRITIONAL NOTES
Per portion:

Energy	142Kcals/600kJ
Fat, total	2.5g
Saturated fat	1.4g
Cholesterol	15.8mg
Fibre	1.5g

4 Pare the rind very thinly from the remaining fruit and set it aside. Cut the pared clementine rind into shreds.

5 Using a sharp knife, cut between the membrane and fruit to separate the citrus segments. Discard the membrane.

6 Place half the segments in four dessert glasses and cover with some of the liquid fruit jelly. Refrigerate to set.

7 Arrange the remaining segments on top. Pour over the remaining liquid jelly and chill until set.

8 Serve topped with crème fraîche sprinkled with clementine rind shreds.

VARIATION
Use ruby grapefruit instead of clementines, if you prefer. Squeeze the juice from half and segment the rest.

FRESH CITRUS JELLY

Fresh fruit jellies really are worth the effort – they're packed with fresh flavour,
natural colour and vitamins – and they make a lovely fat-free dessert.

INGREDIENTS

3 medium oranges
1 lemon
1 lime
300ml/½ pint/1¼ cups water
*75g/3oz/6 tbsp golden caster
(superfine) sugar*
15ml/1 tbsp powdered gelatine
*extra slices of citrus fruit,
to decorate*

SERVES 4

1 Peel one orange and remove all the
white pith with a sharp knife. Cut out the
segments. Discard the membrane.

2 Arrange the segments in the base of a
900ml/1½ pint/3¾ cup mould. Chill.

3 Remove some shreds of citrus rind with
a zester and set aside for decoration.
Grate the remaining rind from the lemon,
the lime and one orange.

COOK'S TIP

To speed up the setting of the fruit
segments in jelly, stand the dish in a
bowl of ice. Or, simply stir the
segments into the liquid jelly, pour into
a serving dish and set it all together.

4 Place the grated rind in a medium pan,
with the water and sugar. Heat gently,
without boiling, until the sugar has
dissolved. Remove from the heat.

5 Squeeze the juice from all the rest
of the fruit and stir it into the pan.

6 Strain the liquid into a measuring jug
(cup) to remove the rind. You should have
about 600ml/1 pint/2½ cups of liquid;
make up the amount with hot water.

7 Sprinkle the gelatine over the liquid
and stir until it has dissolved completely.

8 Pour a little of the jelly over the orange
segments and chill until set.

9 Leave the remaining jelly at room
temperature to cool, but do not allow it
to set.

10 Pour the remaining cooled jelly into
the dish and chill until set.

11 To serve, turn out the jelly and
decorate it with the reserved citrus rind
shreds and extra slices of citrus fruit.

NUTRITIONAL NOTES
Per portion:

Energy	137Kcals/580kJ
Fat, total	0.2g
Saturated fat	0g
Cholesterol	0mg
Fibre	2.1g

DRIED FRUIT SOUP

—

Good-quality dried fruits can be purchased as mixed selections; making them ideal for this recipe. Serve this soup with low-fat Greek yogurt, if you like.

INGREDIENTS

150g/5oz/scant 1 cup mixed dried fruit
1 litre/1¾ pints/4 cups water
100g/3¾ oz/generous ½ cup sugar
1 cinnamon stick
15ml/1 tbsp potato flour
15ml/1 tbsp lemon juice
low-fat Greek (US strained plain) yogurt,
to serve

SERVES 4

1 Put the dried fruit, water and sugar in a pan and leave to soak overnight or for about 12 hours.

2 Add the cinnamon stick to the pan, bring to the boil, then lower the heat and simmer for 15 minutes. Remove and dicard the cinnamon. Using a slotted spoon, transfer the fruit to a serving bowl.

3 Put the potato flour in a bowl and add enough water to form a paste.

4 Bring the cooking liquid to the boil, then stir a little into the paste. Add the potato flour mixture to the pan and, whisking all the time, bring to the boil until lightly thickened. Add the lemon juice, then pour into a serving bowl and leave to cool. Serve cold.

COOK'S TIP

Potato flour is often sold under its French or Italian names, such as "fecule de pommes de terre", or "farina di patate". Cornflour (cornstarch) can be substituted, if you like.

NUTRITIONAL NOTES

Per portion:

Energy	213Kcals/908kJ
Fat, total	0.2g
Saturated fat	0g
Cholesterol	0mg
Fibre	0.9g

GRAPE CHEESE WHIPS

—

A deliciously cool dessert of low-fat cheese and honey, topped with sugar-frosted grapes as decoration that is not to sweet.

INGREDIENTS

150g/5oz/1¹/4 cups black or green seedless grapes, plus tiny bunches, to decorate
2 egg whites
15ml/1 tbsp caster (superfine) sugar
finely grated rind and juice of ¹/2 lemon
225g/8oz/1 cup low-fat soft cheese
45ml/3 tbsp clear honey
30ml/2 tbsp brandy (optional)

SERVES 4

NUTRITIONAL NOTES

Per portion:

Energy	135Kcals/563kJ
Fat, total	3g
Saturated fat	1.2g
Cholesterol	0.56mg
Fibre	0g

1 Brush the tiny bunches of grapes lightly with egg white and sprinkle with sugar to coat. Leave to dry.

2 In a bowl, mix together the lemon rind and juice, cheese, honey and brandy if using. Chop the remaining grapes and stir them into the mixture.

3 Whisk the egg whites in a grease-free bowl until stiff enough to hold soft peaks.

4 Fold the whites into the grape mixture, then spoon into serving glasses.

5 Top with the sugar-frosted grapes and serve chilled.

VARIATION

In place of the grapes use the same quantity of diced peaches or nectarines.

ZABAGLIONE

—

A much-loved, simple and very delicious Italian dessert traditionally made with Marsala,
an Italian fortified wine, although Madeira is a good alternative.

INGREDIENTS
4 egg yolks
50g/2oz/¼ cup sugar
60ml/4 tbsp/¼ cup Marsala or Madeira
amaretti, to serve (optional)

SERVES 6

1 Place the egg yolks and sugar in a
large, clean, heatproof bowl. Beat with an
electric beater until the mixture is pale
and thick and forms fluffy peaks when the
beaters are lifted.

2 Gradually add the Marsala or Madeira,
beating well after each addition.

VARIATION
If you don't have any Marsala or
Madeira, you could use a medium-
sweet sherry or a dessert wine.

3 Now place the bowl over a pan of gently
simmering water and continue to beat for
at least 5–7 minutes, until the mixture
becomes thick and mousse-like.

4 Pour into six warmed small glasses
with stems, such as wine glasses, and
serve immediately with the amaretti for
dipping, if desired.

NUTRITIONAL NOTES
Per portion:

Energy	93 cals
Total fat	4.1g
Saturated fat	1.2g
Cholesterol	150.9mg
Fibre	0g

APPLE FOAM WITH BLACKBERRIES

This lovely light dish is perfect if you fancy a dessert, but don't want anything too rich or too filling. You could use other seasonal berries for this recipe.

INGREDIENTS

225g/8oz/2 cups blackberries
150ml/¼ pint/⅔ cup unsweetened
apple juice
5ml/1 tsp powdered gelatine
15ml/1 tbsp clear honey
2 egg whites

SERVES 4

1 Place the blackberries in a pan with 60ml/4 tbsp of the apple juice and heat gently until the fruit is soft. Remove from the heat, cool, then chill.

2 Sprinkle the gelatine over the remaining apple juice in a small pan and stir over low heat until dissolved. Stir in the honey.

3 In a clean, grease-free bowl, whisk the egg whites until they have more than doubled in volume and hold stiff peaks when the beaters are lifted.

4 Continue whisking hard and pour in the hot gelatine mixture in a slow, steady stream, until well mixed.

5 Quickly spoon the foam into mounds on individual plates. Chill. Serve with the blackberries and juice spooned around.

NUTRITIONAL NOTES
Per portion:

Energy	49Kcals/206kJ
Fat, total	0.2g
Saturated fat	0g
Cholesterol	0mg
Fibre	1.7g

ORANGE YOGURT BRÛLÉES

These are luxurious treats, which are much lower in fat than classic brûlées. They are also quick
to make and ideal for when you wish to serve individual portions.

INGREDIENTS

2 oranges

*150ml/¼ pint/⅔ cup low-fat
Greek (US strained plain) yogurt*

60ml/4 tbsp half-fat crème fraîche

*45ml/3 tbsp golden caster
(superfine) sugar*

*30ml/2 tbsp light muscovado
(brown) sugar*

SERVES 4

1 With a sharp knife, cut away all the
peel and white pith from the oranges and
chop the fruit.

2 Place the fruit in the bottom of four
individual flameproof dishes. Mix
together the yogurt and crème fraîche and
spoon the mixture over the oranges.

3 Mix together the two types of sugars
and sprinkle them evenly over the tops of
the dishes.

4 Place the dishes under a preheated,
very hot grill (broiler) for 3–4 minutes or
until the sugar melts and turns to a rich
golden brown. Serve warm or cold.

NUTRITIONAL NOTES
Per portion:

Energy	154Kcals/648kJ
Fat, total	3.8g
Saturated fat	2.35g
Cholesterol	15.8mg
Fibre	1.4g

CHOCOLATE VANILLA TIMBALES

Not only does this dessert look delicious, it tastes fabulous too, and since it is low in fat and low in calories it is perfect to serve to chocoholic friends.

INGREDIENTS
*350ml/12fl oz/1¹/2 cups
skimmed milk
30ml/2 tbsp unsweetened cocoa powder,
plus extra, for sprinkling
2 eggs, separated
5ml/1 tsp pure vanilla extract
45ml/3 tbsp caster (superfine) sugar
15ml/1 tbsp powdered gelatine
45ml/3 tbsp hot water*

FOR THE SAUCE
*120ml/4fl oz/¹/2 cup low-fat Greek
(US strained plain) yogurt
2.5ml/¹/2 tsp vanilla extract*

SERVES 6

1 Mix the milk and cocoa in a pan; stir over a moderate heat until the milk boils.

2 Beat the egg yolks with the vanilla and sugar in a bowl, until smooth. Pour the chocolate milk in to the egg mixture in a steady stream, beating constantly.

3 Return the mixture to the pan and stir constantly over a gentle heat, without boiling, until it thickens slightly and is smooth.

4 Dissolve the gelatine in the hot water and then quickly stir it into the milk mixture. Cool until at the point of setting.

5 Whisk the egg whites in a grease-free bowl until they hold soft peaks. Fold them quickly into the chocolate milk mixture.

6 Divide the mixture among six individual moulds. Chill until set. Run a knife around the edge of each mould, dip the moulds quickly into hot water and turn out on to serving plates.

7 To make the sauce, stir the yogurt and vanilla extract together, then spoon on to the plates. Sprinkle the sauce with cocoa powder just before serving.

NUTRITIONAL NOTES
Per portion:

Energy	118Kcals/497kJ
Fat, total	4.1g
Saturated fat	1.89g
Cholesterol	66.7mg
Fibre	0.7g

YOGURT WITH APRICOTS AND PISTACHIOS

If you allow yogurt to drain overnight, it becomes thicker and more luscious. Add honeyed apricots and nuts, and you have an exotic yet simple dessert.

INGREDIENTS

*250ml/8fl oz/1 cup low-fat Greek
(US strained plain) yogurt
250ml/8fl oz/1 cup low-fat
natural (plain) yogurt
175g/6oz/3/4 cup ready-to-eat dried
apricots, chopped
15ml/1 tbsp clear honey
10ml/2 tsp unsalted pistachio nuts,
roughly chopped, plus extra for sprinkling
ground cinnamon, for sprinkling*

SERVES 4

1 Mix the yogurts and place in a sieve (strainer) over a bowl. Drain overnight in the refrigerator. Discard the yogurt whey.

2 Place the apricots in a pan, cover with water and simmer to soften. Drain; cool.

3 Pour into a bowl and stir in the honey.

4 Add the yogurt with the nuts. Spoon into sundae dishes, sprinkle over a little cinnamon and nuts and chill.

NUTRITIONAL NOTES
Per portion:

Energy	164Kcals/689kJ
Fat, total	4.5g
Saturated fat	2g
Cholesterol	5.5mg
Fibre	2.8g

DRIED FRUIT FOOL

This light, fluffy dessert can be made with a single type of dried fruit – try dried peaches,
prunes, apples or apricots. Though light and airy, it really is quite filling.

INGREDIENTS
*300g/11oz/1¼ cups ready-to-eat
dried fruit such as apricots, peaches,
prunes or apples
300ml/½ pint/1¼ cups fresh orange juice
250ml/8fl oz/1 cup low-fat ricotta cheese
2 egg whites
fresh mint sprigs, to decorate*

SERVES 4

1 Put the dried fruit in a pan, add the
orange juice and heat gently until boiling.
Lower the heat, cover and simmer for
3 minutes. The fruit will absorb the liquid.

2 Allow the fruit to cool slightly. Transfer
to a food processor or blender and process
until it forms a smooth paste. Stir in the
fromage frais.

3 Whisk the egg whites in a grease-free
bowl until stiff enough to hold soft peaks.

NUTRITIONAL NOTES
Per portion:

Energy	180Kcals/757kJ
Fat, total	0.63g
Saturated fat	0.06g
Cholesterol	0.5mg
Fibre	4.8g

4 Fold the meringue into the fruit mixture
until it is all combined.

5 Spoon the fruit fool into four stemmed
glasses. Chill for at least 1 hour. Decorate
with the mint sprigs just before serving.

COOK'S TIP
To make a speedier fool leave out the
egg whites and simply swirl together
the fruit mixture and fromage frais.
However, the resulting mixture will be
less light and fluffy.

HOT BLACKBERRY AND APPLE SOUFFLÉS

—

As the blackberry season is so short and the apple season so long, it's always worth freezing a
batch of blackberries to have on hand for treats like this one.

3 Put a spoonful of the fruit purée into
each prepared dish and smooth the
surface. Set the dishes aside.

4 Whisk the egg whites in a clean,
grease-free bowl until they form stiff
peaks. Gradually whisk in the remaining
caster sugar to make a stiff, glossy
meringue mixture.

5 Fold in the remaining fruit purée and
spoon the flavoured meringue into the
prepared dishes. Level the tops with a
metal spatula, and run a table knife
around the edge of each dish.

6 Place the dishes on the hot baking
sheet. Bake for 10–15 minutes until the
soufflés have risen and are golden.

7 Dust the tops with icing sugar and
serve immediately.

INGREDIENTS
low-fat spread, for greasing
150g/5oz/2/3 cup caster (superfine) sugar,
plus extra for dusting
350g/12oz/3 cups blackberries
1 large cooking apple, peeled, cored
and finely diced
grated rind and juice of 1 orange
3 egg whites
icing (confectioners') sugar, for dusting

SERVES 6

1 Preheat the oven to 200°C/400°F/Gas 6.
Grease six 150ml/1/4 pint/2/3 cup soufflé
dishes and dust with caster sugar. Put a
baking sheet in the oven to heat.

2 Cook the blackberries and diced apple
with the orange rind and juice in a pan for
10 minutes. Press through a sieve
(strainer) into a bowl. Stir in 50g/2oz/1/4
cup of the caster sugar. Set aside to cool.

COOK'S TIP
Running a table knife around the edge
of the soufflés before baking helps
them to rise evenly without any part
sticking to the rim of the dishes.

NUTRITIONAL NOTES
Per portion:

Energy	138Kcals/584kJ
Fat, total	0.3g
Saturated fat	0.5g
Cholesterol	0mg
Fibre	2.7g

SOUFFLÉED ORANGE SEMOLINA

—

If your opinion of semolina is coloured by the memory of sloppy school puddings, treat yourself to a taste of this sophisticated version.

INGREDIENTS

50g/2oz/¹/4 cup semolina

*600ml/1 pint/2¹/2 cups semi-skimmed
(low-fat) milk*

30ml/2 tbsp muscovado (molasses) sugar

1 large orange

1 egg white

SERVES 4

NUTRITIONAL NOTES

Per portion:

Energy	158Kcals/665kJ
Fat, total	2.67g
Saturated fat	1.54g
Cholesterol	10.5mg
Fibre	0.86g

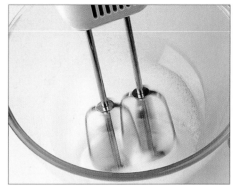

3 Scrub the orange. Pare a few long shreds of rind and save for decoration. Finely grate the rest of the rind.

4 Cut all the peel and white pith from the orange and separate the flesh into equal segments. Stir the segments into the semolina, with the orange rind.

5 Whisk the egg white in a grease-free bowl until stiff but not dry, then fold lightly and evenly into the mixture.

6 Spoon into a 1 litre/1³⁄4 pint/4 cup ovenproof dish and bake for 15–20 minutes, until risen and golden. Scatter over the orange shreds and serve at once.

1 Preheat the oven to 200°C/400°F/Gas 6.

2 Put the semolina in a pan and add the milk and sugar. Stir over a moderate heat until thickened and smooth. Remove from the heat.

COOK'S TIP

When using the rind of citrus fruit, scrub the fruit thoroughly before use, or buy unwaxed fruit.

SOUFFLÉED RICE PUDDING

—

The fluffy egg whites in this unusually light rice pudding make the portions seem much more substantial, without adding lots of extra fat.

INGREDIENTS

65g/2¹/2 oz/¹/3 cup short-grain (pudding) rice
45ml/3 tbsp clear honey
750ml/1¹/4 pints/3 cups semi-skimmed (low-fat) milk
1 vanilla pod (bean) or 2.5ml/¹/2 tsp vanilla extract
2 egg whites
5ml/1 tsp freshly grated nutmeg

SERVES 4

1 Place the rice, honey and milk in a heavy pan and bring the milk to the boil. Add the vanilla pod, if using.

VARIATION

If you like, use skimmed instead of semi-skimmed (low-fat) milk for an even lower-fat dessert.

NUTRITIONAL NOTES

Per portion:

Energy	186Kcals/782kJ
Fat, total	3.7g
Saturated fat	1.88g
Cholesterol	13.1mg
Fibre	0g

2 Lower the heat, cover and simmer over the lowest possible heat for approximately 1–1¹/4 hours, stirring occasionally to prevent sticking, until most of the liquid has been absorbed.

3 Remove the vanilla pod, or, if using vanilla extract, add this to the rice mixture now.

4 Set the pan aside, so that the mixture cools slightly. Preheat the oven to 220°C/425°F/Gas 7.

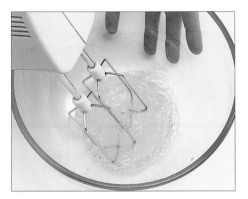

5 Place the egg whites in a clean, grease-free bowl and whisk them until they hold soft peaks when the whisk beaters are lifted.

6 Using a metal spoon, fold the egg whites evenly into the rice mixture, then pour it into a 1 litre/1³/4 pint/4 cup ovenproof dish.

7 Sprinkle the surface with grated nutmeg and bake for 15–20 minutes, until the pudding has risen well and is golden brown. Serve hot or cold.

CINNAMON AND APRICOT SOUFFLÉS

Although this is a soufflé, it really couldn't be easier to make, and it looks and tastes divine.
The flavours complement each other perfectly.

INGREDIENTS

low-fat spread, for greasing
plain (all-purpose) flour, for dusting
3 eggs, separated
115g/4oz/1/2 cup apricot jam
finely grated rind of 1/2 lemon
5ml/1 tsp ground cinnamon, plus extra
to decorate

SERVES 4

NUTRITIONAL NOTES

Per portion:

Energy	134Kcals/560kJ
Fat, total	4.1g
Saturated fat	1.15g
Cholesterol	144.4mg
Fibre	0g

1 Preheat the oven to 190°C/375°F/Gas 5.
Lightly grease four individual soufflé
dishes and dust them lightly with flour.

COOK'S TIP

Puréed fresh or well-drained canned
fruit can be used instead of the apricot
jam, but make sure that the mixture
is not too wet or the soufflés will not
rise properly.

2 Place the egg yolks in a bowl with the
jam, lemon rind and cinnamon.

3 Whisk hard until the mixture is thick
and pale in colour.

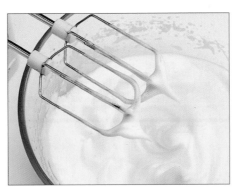

4 Place the egg whites in a grease-free
bowl and whisk them until they form soft
peaks when the whisk is lifted.

VARIATION

Other fruit jams would be delicious in
this soufflé. Try peach or blueberry.

5 Using a metal spoon or spatula,
gradually fold the egg whites into the
yolk mixture.

6 Divide the soufflé mixture among
the prepared dishes.

7 Bake for 10–15 minutes, until
well-risen and golden brown. Serve
immediately, dusted with a little extra
ground cinnamon.

FRUIT SALADS, ICES AND SORBETS

Cool, fresh and colourful – these wonderful combinations of textures and flavours make perfect desserts to follow spicy foods or hearty meals. If time is of the essence, this chapter offers the perfect solution for the busy cook, since many of these recipes can be made ahead of time, leaving space in the day to prepare other courses, or to mingle with guests, of course. There are fruit salads of every description that use minimal ingredients but are big on flavour, and there are appealing ice creams and tasty sorbets too. Citrus fruits and dried fruits help ring the changes in the winter months. Fruit juices, alcohol and liqueurs can be added to dried fruits quickly absorbing the liquid and plumping back to shape, and sharp and tangy citrus fruits are perfectly complemented by aromatic spices. Iced oranges presented in orange shells are sure to be a favourite with children and adults alike.

MIXED FRUIT SALAD

A really good fruit salad is always refreshing, especially when it comes bathed in fresh orange
and lemon juices. Use any mixture of fresh seasonal fruits.

1 Pour the fresh orange and lemon juices into a large serving bowl.

2 Prepare all the fruit by washing or peeling them as necessary. Cut them into bite-size pieces. Halve the grapes and remove any seeds.

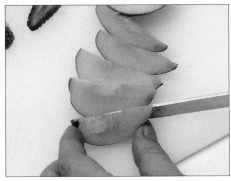

3 Core and slice the apples. Peel them first, if you prefer.

4 Stone (pit) and slice any soft fruits and leave small berries whole. As soon as each fruit is prepared, add it to the juices in the bowl.

5 Taste the salad, adding a sprinkling of sugar if needed. Liqueur can also be added, if you like.

6 Cover the bowl and put it in the refrigerator for at least 2 hours. Mix well and leave to come to room temperature before serving.

INGREDIENTS

juice of 3 large sweet oranges
juice of 1 lemon
1 banana
1–2 apples
1 ripe pear
2 peaches or nectarines
4–5 apricots or plums
115g/4oz/1 cup black or green grapes
115g/4oz/1 cup strawberries, raspberries
or any other fruits in season
sugar, to taste (optional)
30–45ml/2–3 tbsp Kirsch, Maraschino or
other liqueur (optional)

SERVES 4

COOK'S TIP

Try adding chopped fresh herbs such as pineapple mint, lemon balm or borage flowers, to give a herb-infused flavour to this fruit salad.

NUTRITIONAL NOTES
Per portion:

Energy	133Kcals/558kJ
Fat, total	0.4g
Saturated fat	0.03g
Cholesterol	0mg
Fibre	3.8g

FRESH FIGS WITH HONEY AND WINE

**Fresh figs are naturally sweet, and they taste wonderful in a honeyed wine syrup.
Any variety can be used in this recipe, their ripeness determining the cooking time.**

INGREDIENTS

450ml/³/4 pint/scant 2 cups dry white wine
75g/3oz/¹/3 cup clear honey
50g/2oz/¹/4 cup caster (superfine) sugar
1 small orange
8 whole cloves
450g/1lb fresh figs
1 cinnamon stick
bay leaves, to decorate

FOR THE SAUCE

*300ml/¹/2 pint/1¹/4 cups low-fat
Greek (US strained plain) yogurt*
5ml/1 tsp vanilla extract
5ml/1 tsp caster (superfine) sugar

SERVES 6

1 Put the wine, honey and sugar in a heavy pan and heat gently until the sugar dissolves.

2 Stud the orange with the cloves. Add to the syrup with the figs and cinnamon. Cover and simmer until the figs are soft. Transfer to a serving dish. Leave to cool.

3 Flavour the yogurt with the vanilla and sugar. Spoon it into a serving dish.

4 With a small, sharp knife cut one or two of the figs in half, if you like, to show off their pretty centres. Decorate with the bay leaves and serve with the yogurt.

NUTRITIONAL NOTES
Per portion:

Energy	201Kcals/845kJ
Fat, total	2.7g
Saturated fat	1.58g
Cholesterol	3.5mg
Fibre	1.5g

GRAPEFRUIT SALAD WITH CAMPARI AND ORANGE

The bitter-sweet flavour of Campari combines especially well with citrus fruit
for this sophisticated adults-only dessert.

INGREDIENTS
150ml/¹/4 pint/²/3 cup water
45ml/3 tbsp caster (superfine) sugar
60ml/4 tbsp Campari
30ml/2 tbsp lemon juice
4 grapefruit
5 oranges
4 sprigs fresh mint

SERVES 4

COOK'S TIP
When buying citrus fruit, choose
brightly coloured specimens that feel
heavy for their size.

1 Bring the water to the boil in a small
pan, add the sugar and simmer until
dissolved. Fill a large bowl with very cold
water and stand the pan in it to cool the
liquid quickly.

2 Add the Campari and lemon juice.
Chill until ready to serve.

3 Peel the grapefruit and oranges.
Working over a bowl, cut the fruit into
segments. Add them to the bowl, stir in
the Campari syrup and chill again.

4 Spoon the salad into four dishes and
finish with a sprig of fresh mint.

NUTRITIONAL NOTES
Per portion:

Energy	182Kcals/764kJ
Fat, total	0.4g
Saturated fat	0g
Cholesterol	0mg
Fibre	5.3g

FRAGRANT MANDARINS WITH PISTACHIOS

—

Mandarins, tangerines, clementines, mineolas: any of these lovely citrus fruits
could be used for this fragrant and refreshing dessert.

INGREDIENTS
10 mandarins
15ml/1 tbsp icing (confectioners') sugar
10ml/2 tbsp orange-flower water
15ml/1 tbsp chopped pistachio nuts

SERVES 4

1 Pare a little of the mandarin rind and
cut into fine shreds. Squeeze the juice
from two mandarins and set it aside.

2 Peel the remaining fruit, removing all
pith. Arrange the whole fruit in a wide dish.

NUTRITIONAL NOTES
Per portion:

Energy	91Kcals/382kJ
Fat, total	2.2g
Saturated fat	0.25g
Cholesterol	0mg
Fibre	2g

3 Mix the reserved mandarin juice,
icing sugar and orange-flower water and
pour it over the fruit. Cover the dish and
place in the refrigerator for at least an
hour to chill.

4 Blanch the shreds of mandarin rind in
boiling water for 30 seconds. Drain and
cool on kitchen paper, then sprinkle them
over the mandarins, with the pistachio
nuts, and serve.

FRESH FRUIT SALAD AND ALMOND CURD

Also known as Almond Float, this is a wonderfully light Chinese dessert usually made from agar-agar, though gelatine can also be used.

2 In a separate pan, dissolve the sugar in the remaining water over the heat. Add the milk and the almond extract. Blend well, but do not boil.

3 Pour the agar-agar or gelatine mixture into a large serving bowl. Add the flavoured milk gradually, stirring all the time. When cool, refrigerate for 3 hours.

4 To serve, cut the curd into small cubes and spoon into a serving dish. Spoon the fruit salad over the curd and serve.

INGREDIENTS

10g/¹/₄ oz agar-agar or
25g/1oz gelatine
about 600ml/1 pint/2¹/₂ cups water
50g/2oz/¹/₄ cup caster (superfine) sugar
300ml/¹/₂ pint/1¹/₄ cups semi-skimmed
(low-fat) milk
5ml/1 tsp almond extract
fresh fruit salad

SERVES 6

1 In a pan, dissolve the agar-agar (if using) in about half of the water over a gentle heat. This will take at least 10 minutes. If using gelatine, follow the instructions on the sachet.

NUTRITIONAL NOTES
Per portion:

Energy	117Kcals/499kJ
Fat, total	1.2g
Saturated fat	0.75g
Cholesterol	5.3mg
Fibre	0g

ORANGE AND DATE SALAD

—

This Moroccan dessert, made using ingredients popular in North Africa, is simplicity itself, yet it is wonderfully fresh-tasting and light at the end of a rich meal.

INGREDIENTS

6 oranges
15–30ml/1–2 tbsp orange-flower water or rose-water (optional)
lemon juice (optional)
115g/4oz/2/3 cup stoned (pitted) dates
40g/11/2 oz/scant 1/2 cup pistachio nuts
15ml/1 tbsp icing (confectioners') sugar, plus extra for dusting
5ml/1 tsp toasted almonds

SERVES 6

1 Peel the oranges with a sharp knife, removing all the pith. Cut into segments, catching the juice in a bowl. Place in a serving dish.

2 Stir in the juice from the bowl, with a little orange-flower or rose-water, if using, and sharpen with lemon juice, if liked.

3 Chop the dates and pistachio nuts and sprinkle over the salad with the icing sugar. Chill for 1 hour.

4 Just before serving, sprinkle the salad with the toasted almonds and dust with a little extra icing sugar.

NUTRITIONAL NOTES

Per portion:

Energy	147Kcals/616kJ
Fat, total	4.3g
Saturated fat	0.45g
Cholesterol	0mg
Fibre	3.5g

MUSCAT GRAPE FRAPPÉ

The flavour and perfume of the Muscat grape is rarely more enticing than when captured in this icy-cool salad. It's a light and tasty combination that is ideal after a rich meal.

2 Remove the seeds from the grapes with tweezers. Peel the grapes, if you like.

3 Scrape the frozen wine with a tablespoon to make a fine ice. Combine the grapes with the ice and spoon into four shallow glasses.

INGREDIENTS
1/2 bottle Muscat wine, Beaumes de Venise, Frontignan or Rivesaltes
150ml/1/4 pint/2/3 cup water
450g/1lb/4 cups Muscat grapes

SERVES 4

1 Pour the wine into a stainless-steel or non-stick tray, add the water and freeze for 3 hours or until completely solid.

COOK'S TIP
To make this frappé alcohol-free, substitute 300ml/1/2 pint/1 1/4 cups apple or grape juice for the wine.

NUTRITIONAL NOTES
Per portion:

Energy	155Kcals/651kJ
Fat, total	0g
Saturated fat	0g
Cholesterol	0mg
Fibre	1g

MARZIPAN FIGS WITH DATES

—

Sweet Mediterranean figs and dates combine especially well with crisp dessert apples.
A hint of almond serves to unite the flavours.

INGREDIENTS

6 large eating apples
juice of 1/2 lemon
175g/6oz/1 cup fresh dates
25g/1oz white marzipan
5ml/1 tsp orange flower water
60ml/4 tbsp low-fat natural (plain) yogurt
4 green or purple figs
4 almonds, toasted

SERVES 4

1 Core the apples. Slice thinly, then cut into fine matchsticks. Moisten with lemon juice to prevent the matchsticks from browning. Place in a bowl.

2 Remove the stones (pits) from the dates. Cut the flesh into strips. Add to the apple.

3 Soften the marzipan with orange flower water and combine with the low-fat yogurt. Mix well.

4 Pile the apples and dates in the centres of four plates.

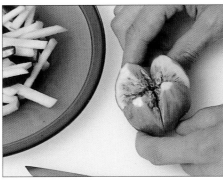

5 Remove the stem from each of the figs and cut into quarters without slicing right through the base. Squeeze the base to open the fruit.

6 Place a fig in the centre of the salad, spoon in the yogurt filling and decorate each portion with a toasted almond.

NUTRITIONAL NOTES

Per portion:

Energy	210Kcals/884kJ
Fat, total	3.1g
Saturated fat	0.15g
Cholesterol	0.6mg
Fibre	5.4g

WINTER FRUIT SALAD

A colourful, refreshing and nutritious fruit salad, this makes an excellent choice
for a winter buffet. It's quick and easy to prepare too.

2 Segment the oranges, catching any
juice in the bowl, then add the orange
segments and pineapple to the fruit
juice mixture.

3 Core and chop the apples and pears
and add them to the bowl.

4 Stir in the plums, dates and apricots.
Cover and chill for several hours.
Decorate with fresh mint sprigs to serve.

INGREDIENTS

225g/8oz can pineapple cubes in fruit juice
200ml/7fl oz/scant 1 cup fresh orange juice
200ml/7fl oz/scant 1 cup unsweetened
apple juice
30ml/2 tbsp orange- or
apple-flavoured liqueur
30ml/2 tbsp clear honey (optional)
2 oranges, peeled
2 green eating apples
2 pears
4 plums, stoned (pitted) and chopped
12 fresh dates, stoned (pitted) and chopped
115g/4oz/1/2 cup ready-to-eat
dried apricots
fresh mint sprigs, to decorate

SERVES 6

1 Drain the pineapple, reserving the juice
in a large serving bowl. Add the orange
juice, apple juice, liqueur and honey, if
using, and stir.

NUTRITIONAL NOTES
Per portion:

Energy	227Kcals/967kJ
Fat, total	0.37g
Saturated fat	0g
Cholesterol	0mg
Fibre	5.34g

RUBY FRUIT SALAD

After a rich main course, this port-flavoured fruit salad is light and appealing.
Use any fresh fruit that is available.

INGREDIENTS

300ml/¹/2 pint/1¹/4 cups water
115g/4oz/¹/2 cup caster (superfine) sugar
1 cinnamon stick
4 cloves
pared rind of 1 orange
300ml/¹/2 pint/1¹/4 cups port
2 oranges
*1 small ripe Ogen, Charentais or
honeydew melon*
4 small bananas
2 eating apples
225g/8oz/2 cups seedless grapes

SERVES 8

1 Put the water, sugar, spices and pared orange rind into a pan and stir over a gentle heat to dissolve the sugar. Bring to the boil, lower the heat, cover and simmer for 10 minutes. Leave to cool.

2 Add the port. Strain the liquid into a bowl.

NUTRITIONAL NOTES

Per portion:

Energy	212Kcals/895kJ
Fat, total	0.2g
Saturated fat	0.04g
Cholesterol	0mg
Fibre	1.9g

3 With a sharp knife, cut off all the skin and pith from the oranges. Then, holding each orange over the bowl to catch the juice, cut it into segments, allowing them to drop into the syrup. Squeeze the remaining pulp to release any juice.

4 Cut the melon in half, remove the seeds and scoop out the flesh or cut it in small cubes. Add it to the syrup.

5 Peel the bananas and cut them diagonally in 1cm/¹/2in slices. Quarter and core the apples and cut the wedges into small cubes. Leave the skin on, or peel them if it is tough. Halve the grapes if large or leave them whole.

6 Stir all the fruit into the syrup, cover with clear film and chill for an hour before serving.

BLACKBERRY SALAD WITH ROSE GRANITA

The blackberry is a member of the rose family and combines especially well with rose-water.
Here a rose syrup is frozen into a granita and served over strips of white meringue.

INGREDIENTS
600ml/1 pint/2½ cups water
150g/5oz/⅔ cup caster (superfine) sugar
petals from 1 fresh red rose, finely chopped
5ml/1 tsp rose water
10ml/2 tsp lemon juice
450g/1lb/4 cups blackberries
icing (confectioners') sugar, for dusting

FOR THE MERINGUE
2 egg whites
115g/4oz/½ cup caster (superfine) sugar

SERVES 4

1 Bring 150ml/¼ pint/⅔ cup of the water to the boil in a stainless-steel or enamel pan. Add the sugar and chopped rose petals, then lower the heat and simmer for 5 minutes.

2 Strain the syrup into a deep metal tray, add the remaining water, the rose water and lemon juice; leave to cool. Freeze for approximately 3 hours or until solid.

3 Preheat the oven to 140°C/275°F/Gas 1.

4 Line a baking sheet with six layers of newspaper and cover with non-stick baking paper.

5 To make the meringue, whisk the egg whites in a grease-free bowl until they form soft peaks.

6 Whisk in the caster sugar, a little at a time, then continue to whisk until the meringue forms stiff peaks when the whisk is lifted.

7 Spoon the meringue into a piping bag fitted with a 1cm/½in plain nozzle. Pipe the meringue in lengths across the paper-lined baking sheet. Dry in the bottom of the oven for 1½–2 hours.

8 Break the meringue into 5cm/2in lengths and place three or four lengths on each of four large plates. Pile the blackberries next to the meringue.

9 With a tablespoon, scrape the granita finely. Shape into ovals and place over the meringue. Dust with icing sugar and serve immediately.

NUTRITIONAL NOTES
Per portion:

Energy	310Kcals/1318kJ
Fat, total	0.2g
Saturated fat	0g
Cholesterol	0mg
Fibre	3.5g

COOK'S TIP
Serve the dessert as soon as possible after piling the granita on the meringue, or the meringue will soon become soggy.

VARIATION
Other soft fruits such as blueberries, raspberries or loganberries would work equally well in this dessert. Choose whatever looks juiciest.

APRICOT AND BANANA COMPOTE

This compote is delicious served on its own or with low-fat custard or ice cream. Served for breakfast, it makes a tasty start to the day.

3 Spoon the fruit and juices into a large serving dish.

4 Serve immediately, or cover and chill for several hours first. Sprinkle with flaked almonds just before serving with low-fat custard or ice cream, if you wish.

INGREDIENTS

225g/8oz/1 cup ready-to-eat dried apricots
300ml/¹/₂ pint/1¹/₄ cups unsweetened orange juice
150ml/¹/₄ pint/²/₃ cup unsweetened apple juice
5ml/1 tsp ground ginger
3 medium bananas, sliced
25g/1oz/¹/₄ cup toasted flaked (slivered) almonds
low-fat custard or ice cream, (optional)

SERVES 4

1 Put the apricots in a pan with the fruit juices and ginger and stir. Cover, bring to the boil and then simmer gently for 10 minutes, stirring occasionally. Set aside to go cold, leaving the lid on.

2 Stir in the sliced bananas.

VARIATION
Dried prunes or figs and fresh apples or peaches could be used instead.

NUTRITIONAL NOTES
Per portion:

Energy	241Kcals/1022kJ
Fat, total	4.18g
Saturated fat	0.37g
Cholesterol	0mg
Fibre	4.91g

REDCURRANT PUDDING

—

This fruit pudding from Russia, called Kissel, is traditionally made from the thickened juice of
stewed red- or blackcurrants. This recipe uses the whole fruit with added blackberry liqueur.

INGREDIENTS

*225g/8oz/2 cups red or blackcurrants or
a mixture of both*
225g/8oz/2 cups raspberries
150ml/¼ pint/⅔ cup water
50g/2oz/¼ cup caster (superfine) sugar
25ml/1½ tbsp arrowroot
15ml/1 tbsp blackberry liqueur
*low-fat Greek (US strained plain) yogurt,
to serve (optional)*

SERVES 4

1 Put the currants and raspberries, water
and sugar in a pan. Cover and cook over a
low heat for 12–15 minutes, until the
fruit is soft.

2 Blend the arrowroot to a paste with a
little water in a small bowl and stir into
the hot fruit mixture.

3 Bring the fruit mixture back to the boil,
stirring until thickened and smooth.

4 Remove the pan from the heat and
leave the fruit compote to cool slightly,
then gently stir in the liqueur.

NUTRITIONAL NOTES

Per portion:

Energy	105Kcals/443kJ
Fat, total	0.2g
Saturated fat	0g
Cholesterol	0mg
Fibre	3.3g

5 Pour the compote into four glass
serving bowls and leave until cold, then
chill until required. Serve solo or with
spoonfuls of Greek yogurt, if you like.

COOK'S TIP

Crème de mûre is a French blackberry
liqueur, which is available from large
supermarkets. You could use crème de
cassis, which is blackcurrant liqueur,
instead, if you like.

KUMQUAT COMPOTE

—

Warm, spicy and full of sun-ripened ingredients – this is the perfect winter dessert
to remind you of long summer days.

INGREDIENTS

200g/7oz/2 cups kumquats, washed
*200g/7oz/scant 1 cup ready-to-eat
dried apricots*
30ml/2 tbsp sultanas (golden raisins)
400ml/14fl oz/1²/₃ cups water
1 orange
2.5cm/1in piece of fresh root ginger
4 cardamom pods
4 cloves
30ml/2 tbsp clear honey
*15ml/1 tbsp flaked (sliced)
almonds, toasted*

SERVES 4

1 If the kumquats are large, cut
them in half. Place them in a heavy
pan with the dried apricots, sultanas
and water. Bring to the boil slowly
over a gentle heat.

2 Pare the orange rind. Peel and grate
the ginger and add to the pan. Crush the
cardamom pods and add the seeds, with
the cloves.

3 Reduce the heat, cover the pan and
leave to simmer for 30 minutes, or until
the fruit is tender, stirring occasionally.

4 Squeeze the juice from the orange and
add to the compote. Sweeten with the
honey, sprinkle with the almonds and
serve warm.

NUTRITIONAL NOTES
Per portion:

Energy	198Kcals/833kJ
Fat, total	2.9g
Saturated fat	0.25g
Cholesterol	0mg
Fibre	6.9g

GINGER AND HONEY SYRUP

—

Particularly good for winter puddings, this virtually fat-free sauce can be served hot or cold with a variety of your favourite fruit salads.

INGREDIENTS
1 lemon
4 green cardamom pods
1 cinnamon stick
150ml/¼ pint/²/₃ cup clear honey
3 pieces stem ginger, plus
30ml/2 tbsp syrup from the jar
60ml/4 tbsp water

SERVES 4

1 Thinly pare two strips of rind from the lemon with a potato peeler. Cut the lemon in half. Reserve half for another recipe and squeeze the juice from the other half. Set the juice aside.

2 Lightly crush the cardamom pods with the back of a heavy-bladed knife.

COOK'S TIP
Citrus fruits work well with this recipe.

NUTRITIONAL NOTES
Per portion:

Energy	145Kcals/611kJ
Fat, total	0.1g
Saturated fat	0g
Cholesterol	0mg
Fibre	0g

3 Place the lemon rind, cardamoms, cinnamon stick, honey, ginger syrup and water in a heavy pan. Boil, lower the heat and simmer for 2 minutes.

4 Chop the ginger and stir it into the sauce with the lemon juice. Chill to serve. Pour over a winter fruit salad or try it with a baked fruit compote.

SPICED FRUITS JUBILEE
—

**Based on the classic Cherries Jubilee, this is a great way to use up a glut of any stone fruit.
The spiced syrup is a delicious bonus.**

3 Add the fruit, cover the pan and simmer for 5 minutes.

4 Drain the fruit and set it aside; return the syrup to the pan. Boil it, uncovered, for 2 minutes or until thick and syrupy.

5 Put the arrowroot in a small bowl and stir in 30ml/2 tbsp of the brandy. Stir the mixture into the syrup. Continue cooking and stirring, until the sauce thickens. Return the fruit to the pan.

6 If serving with ice cream, place a scoop in each serving bowl and spoon the hot fruit over.

7 Warm the remaining brandy in a small pan, then set it alight. Ladle it over the fruit at the table for maximum dramatic effect.

INGREDIENTS

115g/4oz/1/2 cup caster (superfine) sugar
thinly pared rind of 1 lemon
1 cinnamon stick
4 whole cloves
300ml/1/2 pint/11/4 cups water
*225g/8oz tart red plums, stoned (pitted)
and sliced*
*225g/8oz nectarines, stoned (pitted)
and chopped*
225g/8oz/2 cups cherries, stoned (pitted)
5ml/1 tsp arrowroot
75ml/5 tbsp brandy
*low-fat vanilla ice cream, to serve
(optional)*

SERVES 6

1 Put the sugar, lemon rind, cinnamon stick, cloves and water in a pan. Bring to the boil, stirring. Lower the heat and simmer for 5 minutes.

2 Lift out the spices with a slotted spoon and discard.

NUTRITIONAL NOTES
Per portion:

Energy	151Kcals/639kJ
Fat, total	0.1g
Saturated fat	0g
Cholesterol	0mg
Fibre	1g

ITALIAN FRUIT SALAD AND ICE CREAM

If you visit Italy in the summer, you will find little pavement fruit shops selling small dishes of macerated soft fruits, which are delectable on their own, but also make a wonderful ice cream.

INGREDIENTS

900g/2lb/8 cups mixed soft fruits, such as strawberries, raspberries, loganberries, redcurrants, blueberries, peaches, apricots, plums and melons
juice of 6–8 oranges
juice of 1 lemon
15ml/1 tbsp liquid pear and apple concentrate
60ml/4 tbsp very low-fat fromage frais
30ml/2 tbsp orange-flavoured liqueur (optional)
fresh mint sprigs, to decorate

SERVES 6

1 Prepare the fruit according to type. Cut it into bite-size pieces. Put the fruit pieces in a serving bowl.

2 Pour over enough orange juice to cover the fruit. Add the lemon juice, stir gently, cover and chill in the refrigerator for 2 hours.

3 Set half the fruit aside to serve as it is. Purée the remainder in a blender or food processor.

4 Gently warm the pear and apple concentrate and stir it into the fruit purée. Whip the fromage frais and fold it in, then add the liqueur, if using.

NUTRITIONAL NOTES
Per portion:

Energy	60Kcals/254kJ
Fat, total	0.2g
Saturated fat	0.01g
Cholesterol	0.1mg
Fibre	3.2g

5 Place in a container and freeze it until ice crystals form around the edge.

6 Beat the mixture until smooth. Repeat the process once or twice, then freeze until firm. Serve decorated with mint and accompanied by the reserved fruit.

ICED ORANGES

These tasty little sorbets served in the fruit shell look impressive and are easy to eat – just the thing for serving for a light Christmas-time dessert.

INGREDIENTS
150g/5oz/²⁄3 cup sugar
juice of 1 lemon
200ml/7fl oz/scant 1 cup water
14 oranges
8 fresh bay leaves, to decorate

SERVES 8

NUTRITIONAL NOTES
Per portion:

Energy	167Kcals/703kJ
Fat, total	0.3g
Saturated fat	0g
Cholesterol	0mg
Fibre	4.3g

1 Put the sugar in a heavy pan. Add half the lemon juice, then pour in 120ml/4fl oz/½ cup of the water. Heat gently, stirring occasionally, until the sugar has dissolved, then bring to the boil, and boil for 2–3 minutes, until the syrup is clear. Leave to cool.

2 Slice the tops off eight of the oranges, to make 'hats'. Scoop out the flesh from inside each one, taking care not to damage the shell, and set it aside. Put the empty orange shells and the 'hats' on a baking sheet and place in the freezer until needed.

3 Grate the rind of the six remaining oranges and add this to the syrup. Squeeze the juice from the oranges, and from the reserved flesh. There should be 750ml/1¼ pints/3 cups. Top up with water, if necessary.

4 Stir the orange juice into the syrup, with the remaining lemon juice and water. Pour the mixture into a shallow container that can safely be used in the freezer. Freeze for 3 hours.

5 Turn the mixture into a bowl, and whisk to break down the ice crystals. Return to the freezer container and freeze for 4 hours more, until firm, but not solid.

6 Pack the mixture into the orange shells, mounding it up, and set the 'hats' on top. Freeze until ready to serve. Just before serving, make a hole in the top of each 'hat', using a skewer, and push in a bay leaf as decoration.

COOK'S TIP
Use crumpled foil wrapped around the oranges individually to keep the shells upright on the baking sheet while they are in the freezer.

CHRISTMAS CRANBERRY BOMBE
———

This alternative to Christmas pudding is light and low in fat, but still very festive and luxurious.
Make it when cranberries are plentiful and economic to buy.

INGREDIENTS
250ml/8fl oz/1 cup buttermilk
60ml/4 tbsp low-fat crème fraîche
1 vanilla pod (bean)
2 eggs
30ml/2 tbsp clear honey
30ml/2 tbsp chopped angelica
30ml/2 tbsp mixed (candied) peel
10ml/2 tsp flaked (slivered)
almonds, toasted

FOR THE SORBET CENTRE
175g/6oz/1¹/₂ cups fresh or
frozen cranberries
150ml/¹/₄ pint/²/₃ cup fresh orange juice
finely grated rind of ¹/₂ orange
2.5ml/¹/₂ tsp mixed (apple pie) spice
50g/2oz/¹/₄ cup golden caster
(superfine) sugar

SERVES 6

1 Heat the buttermilk, crème fraîche and vanilla pod in a pan until almost boiling. Remove the vanilla pod.

2 Place the eggs in a heatproof bowl set over a pan of hot water and whisk until they are pale and thick.

3 Pour in the buttermilk in a thin stream, whisking until the mixture thickens slightly. Whisk in the honey. Cool.

NUTRITIONAL NOTES
Per portion:

Energy	153Kcals/644kJ
Fat, total	4.6g
Saturated fat	1.58g
Cholesterol	75.5mg
Fibre	1.5g

4 Spoon into a freezer container and freeze until slushy. Stir in the chopped angelica, mixed peel and almonds.

5 Pack into a pudding basin and hollow out the centre. Freeze until firm.

6 To make the sorbet, put the cranberries, orange juice, rind and spice in a pan and cook gently until the cranberries are soft. Set some cranberries aside for decorating.

7 Add the sugar to the rest, then purée in a food processor until almost smooth. Leave to cool.

8 Fill the hollowed-out centre of the basin with the cranberry mixture, smooth over and freeze until firm.

9 To serve, allow to soften slightly, then turn out and serve in slices, decorated with the reserved cranberries.

FROZEN APPLE AND BLACKBERRY TERRINE

Apples and blackberries are a classic autumn combination; they really complement each other.
This pretty, three-layered terrine can be frozen, so you can enjoy it at any time of year.

INGREDIENTS

450g/1lb cooking or eating apples
300ml/½ pint/1¼ cups sweet (hard) cider
15ml/1 tbsp clear honey
5ml/1 tsp vanilla extract
*200g/7oz/scant 2 cups fresh or frozen and
thawed blackberries*
15ml/1 tbsp powdered gelatine
2 egg whites
*fresh apple slices and blackberries,
to decorate*

SERVES 6

1 Peel, core and chop the apples and place them in a pan with half the cider. Bring the cider to the boil, then lower the heat, cover the pan and let the apples simmer gently until tender.

COOK'S TIPS

• For a quick version the mixture can be set without the layering. Purée the apples and blackberries together, stir the dissolved gelatine and whisked egg whites into the mixture, turn the whole thing into the tin (pan) and leave to set.
• Red grape juice has a good flavour and improves the colour of the ice, but if it is not available, use cranberry, apple or orange juice instead.

2 Transfer the apples to a food processor and process to a smooth purée. Stir in the honey and vanilla. Decant half to a bowl.

3 Add half the blackberries to the purée, in the processor and process again until smooth. Sieve (strain) to remove the pips.

4 Heat the remaining cider until almost boiling, then sprinkle the gelatine over and stir until dissolved. Add half the gelatine mixture to the apple purée and half to the blackberry purée.

NUTRITIONAL NOTES
Per portion:

Energy	83Kcals/346kJ
Fat, total	0.2g
Saturated fat	0g
Cholesterol	0mg
Fibre	2.6g

5 Leave both purées to cool until almost set.

6 Whisk the egg whites until they are stiff. Quickly fold them into the apple purée. Decant half the purée into a bowl.

7 Stir the remaining whole blackberries into apple purée in the bowl, and then pour this into a 1.75 litre/3 pint/7½ cup loaf tin (pan), packing it down firmly.

8 Top with the blackberry purée and spread it evenly.

9 Add the plain apple purée and smooth it evenly. If necessary, freeze each layer until firm before adding the next.

10 Freeze the terrine until firm. Before serving, allow to stand at room temperature for about 20 minutes to soften. Serve in slices, decorated with apple slices and blackberries.

PLUM AND PORT SORBET

—

Rather a grown-up sorbet, this one, but you could use still red grape juice
instead of port if you prefer.

INGREDIENTS
*900g/2lb ripe red plums, halved
and stoned (pitted)
75g/3oz/6 tbsp caster (superfine) sugar
45ml/3 tbsp water
45ml/3 tbsp ruby port or red wine
crisp, sweet biscuits, to serve (optional)*

SERVES 6

1 Put the plums in a pan with the sugar
and water. Stir over a gentle heat until the
sugar has melted, then cover and simmer
gently for about 5 minutes, until the fruit
is soft.

2 Pour into a food processor and purée
until smooth, then stir in the port or wine,
but check first that all the stones (pits)
have been removed from the fruit.

3 Allow to cool completely, then transfer
to a freezer-proof container and freeze
until firm around the edges.

4 Spoon into the food processor and
process until smooth. Return to the
freezer and freeze until solid.

5 Soften slightly at room temperature
then serve in scoops, with sweet biscuits
if you like, but they will add fat content.

NUTRITIONAL NOTES
Per portion:

Energy	166Kcals/699kJ
Fat, total	0.25g
Saturated fat	0g
Cholesterol	0mg
Fibre	3.75g

RUBY GRAPEFRUIT SORBET

Grapefruit is particularly refreshing, and this light dessert would be perfect to follow
a meaty main course, to cleanse the palate.

INGREDIENTS

175g/6oz/3/4 cup sugar
120ml/4fl oz/1/2 cup water
1 litre/13/4 pints/4 cups strained freshly
squeezed ruby grapefruit juice
15ml/1 tbsp fresh lemon juice
15ml/1 tbsp icing (confectioners') sugar
mint leaves, to decorate

SERVES 8

1 In a small heavy pan, dissolve the sugar
in the water over a medium heat, without
stirring. When the sugar has dissolved,
boil the syrup for 3–4 minutes. Remove
from the heat and leave to cool.

2 Pour the cooled sugar syrup into the
grapefruit juice. Stir well.

3 Taste the mixture and adjust the flavour
by adding the lemon juice or the icing
sugar, if necessary.

NUTRITIONAL NOTES
Per portion:

Energy	133Kcals/568kJ
Fat, total	0.1g
Saturated fat	0g
Cholesterol	0mg
Fibre	0g

4 Pour the mixture into a metal or plastic
freezer container and freeze for about
3 hours, or until softly set.

5 Remove from the container and chop
roughly into 7.5cm/3in pieces. Place in a
food processor and process until smooth.
Return the mixture to the freezer
container and freeze again until set.
Repeat this freezing and chopping
process 2 or 3 times, until a smooth
consistency is obtained.

6 Alternatively, freeze the sorbet in
an ice-cream maker, following the
manufacturer's instructions. Serve,
decorated with mint leaves.

FRESH ORANGE GRANITA

A granita is like a water ice, but coarser and quite grainy in texture, hence its name.
It makes a refreshing dessert after a rich main course.

INGREDIENTS
4 large oranges
1 large lemon
150g/5oz/2/3 cup sugar
475ml/16fl oz/2 cups water
dessert biscuits, to serve (optional)
pared strips of orange and lemon rind,
to decorate

SERVES 6

1 Thinly pare the orange and lemon rind, avoiding the white pith, and set aside for the decoration. Cut the fruit in half and squeeze the juice into a jug. Set aside.

2 Heat the sugar and water in a heavy pan, stirring, until the sugar dissolves. Bring to the boil, then boil without stirring, until a syrup forms. Remove the syrup from the heat, add the pieces of orange and lemon rind and shake the pan. Cover and allow to cool.

NUTRITIONAL NOTES
Per portion:

Energy	139Kcals/589kJ
Fat, total	0.2g
Saturated fat	0g
Cholesterol	0mg
Fibre	1.6g

3 Strain the sugar syrup into a shallow freezer container and add the fruit juice. Stir well to mix, then freeze, uncovered, for about 4 hours until slushy.

COOK'S TIP
To make the decoration, slice extra orange and lemon rind into thin strips. Blanch for 2 minutes, refresh under cold water and dry before use.

4 Remove the half-frozen mixture from the freezer and mix with a fork, then return to the freezer and freeze again for 4 hours more or until frozen solid.

5 To serve, turn into a bowl and leave to soften for about 10 minutes, then break up again and pile into long-stemmed glasses. Decorate with the strips of orange and lemon rind. Serve with dessert biscuits, if you like, but remember to take their fat content into account.

INDEX